Equality,
Liberty's Lost Twin

Equality, Liberty's Lost Twin

A Short History of Ideas from Rousseau to Rawls

Kenneth L. Penegar

Algora Publishing
New York

Library of Congress Cataloging-in-Publication Data —

Names: Penegar, Kenneth Lawing, author.
Title: Equality: liberty's lost twin: A short history of ideas from Rousseau to Rawls /
Kenneth L. Penegar.
Description: New York: Algora Publishing, [2021] | Includes
    bibliographical references. | Summary: "Inequality seems to be the only
    topic under discussion today. But what do we actually mean by equality,
    and what did the American Founders have in mind? This work, a history of
    ideas and at the same time a parallel study of social and political
    dimensions, is intended for college educators, commentators and public
    officials"— Provided by publisher.
Identifiers: LCCN 2020048423 (print) | LCCN 2020048424 (ebook) | ISBN
    9781628944228 (Trade Paperback) | ISBN 9781628944235 (Hardcover) | ISBN
    9781628944242 (PDF)
Subjects: LCSH: Equality—United States—History. | Political
    science—United States—History. | Social justice.
Classification: LCC JC575 .P395 2021 (print) | LCC JC575 (ebook) | DDC
    320.01/1—dc23
LC record available at https://lccn.loc.gov/2020048423
LC ebook record available at https://lccn.loc.gov/2020048424

Printed in the United States

I dedicate this book to the memory of my late brother Richard Penegar (1930–2016), who lived all his life with the certainty that everyone he knew or met was worthy of his respect. He showed that when he helped a youngster or fledging business reach just beyond where they might have imagined. He showed it also when he fostered new ways to re-weave a city's sense of shared belonging—in a school, or civic club, or church. Somehow, through a time and in a community historically shadowed by separation, Richard found it possible to promote unity by celebrating diversity.

The book is dedicated also to my wife and kindred spirit, Anne Bankhead Lane. Her resourceful mind and talents of expression added their own depth to the project. An unlimited patience reinforced Anne's many specific contributions. During several years of research and writing, my continuing pre-occupation often challenged routines of household and social activity. Yet her interest in the book's progress remained strong and steady. Momentum was sustained by the numerous discussions we had about the book's themes and people. It is difficult for me to imagine how the book could have come to be without Anne's distinctive investment in it.

Table of Contents

INTRODUCTION

In the summer of 1998, the *Wall Street Journal* carried on its front page the account of an unusual fiftieth high school reunion. The graduates of two schools, one Black, one White, who had not attended classes together as students, decided as adults to cross that old line and meet as citizens of a new time.[1]

Thinking about that newsworthy story spawned a cascade of memories of the time when "separate but equal" was all the law allowed in the South.[2] In my senior year of college, the Supreme Court overturned *Plessy v. Ferguson* and many of us cheered a new era. Two years before that, an organization in North Carolina called the State Student Legislature (SSL) met in the state capital and authored a bill calling for an end to state-enforced segregation; it passed by a significant majority.

Membership in the SSL, open to all colleges in the state, included significant numbers of fledgling "legislators" from Black colleges, too. No one publicly noted the irony of a racially integrated meeting that would have been unlawful on any of their respective campuses. Little did any of us know, even after *Brown v Board*, in 1954, that actual desegregation would not be realized for years more. Little Rock, Arkansas, refused in 1957 to obey a court order to desegregate schools, so President Eisenhower ordered federal marshals, backed by active units of the National Guard, into the city. Most extreme was the reaction of Prince Edward County, Virginia, where they closed their

---

[1] Roger Thurow, "After 50 Years, Some Try to Lay the Ghosts Of Segregation to Rest," *The Wall Street Journal*, June 8, 1998.

[2] No doubt the memory in and of that story is more vivid for some than others, for the town was my own and one of the co-planners of the event was my brother.

public schools rather than allow an end to segregated schools. At least one regional politician called for "massive resistance" to thwart the reach of the Supreme Court's order for the change to proceed with "all deliberate speed."[3]

Not fully a decade later, what became the civil rights movement was well underway with sit-in protests for lunch counter desegregation in Greensboro and Nashville. Most memorable, personally, was Dr. Martin Luther King, Jr.'s "I Have a Dream" speech in 1963 on the steps of the Lincoln Memorial. Working for a federal judge in D.C., I asked for a day of leave to attend, walked up Constitution Avenue, and stood for more than an hour to hear a bracing call for justice to "roll down like water and righteousness like a mighty river" on the nation. No doubt the self-discipline of the huge crowd, stretched as far as the eye could see on both sides of the Reflecting Pool, impressed those present, too, for it seemed to express the character of the movement's commitment to non-violence. The crowd dispersed without incident; police presence was minimal and seemed largely ceremonial.

Forty-plus years after those incidents, the experience of teaching and writing in legal fields sharpened an appetite for a deeper understanding of what a generation experienced and thought, and inspired the inquiries that have become this book. But like amateur archaeologists, those seeking knowledge of one layer below the earth's present surface have to somehow prepare themselves for layers of significance below that. There are interactions and influences that build on one another without clear-cut boundaries between one age and another. The amateur historian has no less a challenge. What ideas lie behind the incidents of temporal politics and demands for social change? How and by whom have these ideas been expressed? "Equal justice under law" as a principal ideal of the American constitutional system clearly had one set—or more—of meanings before the 1960s and a different set, at least partially, for the next generation. What changed and why?

More basic still than the meanings of whole phrases of legal import like "equal justice under law" lie component concepts carried forward culturally and not merely through institutional or professional norms. Standing just outside the legal terms themselves are the beliefs, values, ideals and arguments that shape those terms over time. Just as a protest movement carried forward political reforms in civil rights laws and practices in mid-twentieth century America, thinking seriously about inherited inequalities then gave

---

[3] Ira D. Lechner, "Massive Resistance: Virginia's Great Leap Backward," *Virginia Quarterly Review* 74, (Autumn 1998), 631-40.

rise to new initiatives like affirmative action in college admissions and employment.

Similarly, trends of rising economic disparity over the last four decades have generated widespread analysis by both economists and political scientists, even as politicians have argued over both causes and remedies. We will examine studies of those trends in the last two chapters of this book. To prepare for one's own assessment of them, the majority of chapters will trace main historic paths we seem to have followed. It is a task open to all, the on-again, off-again business of following some one or more of the trails or themes of history. There are not many, however, who can claim their interpretation is authoritative. For most of us, especially those of us who have not gone to primary sources for their evidence, it is but our own selectivity, however constructed, that both informs and limits our summaries. The template, to the extent one can be truly aware of his own, for this book is composed from the very broad themes of political thought as highlighted in such works as Columbia College's *Introduction to Contemporary Civilization in the West.* [4]

The era spanning the last two decades of the twentieth and the first two decades of the twenty-first centuries is one of more anxiety than experiment, more disparagement than consensus. Arguably it is an era, too, when ideological conceits hobble the debate, and partisan posturing characterizes much of the mass media's capacity for following what politicians and experts are saying or doing.

A Word about the Title

The implicit claim in *Liberty's Lost Twin* is that the two ideals are intimately related—even part of the same family. More explicitly the title suggests that somehow Equality has been cut off from or less favored than Liberty. Nonetheless we can identify the course of that ideal by the artifacts of writing and public actions, not to mention their authors and participants.

---

[4] *Introduction to Contemporary Civilization in the West*, edited by Staff of Columbia College, (New York: Columbia University Press, 1946). Formerly, over a generation ago, there was a required course in liberal arts curricula by that or a similar title. If we missed that course, as I did in college, or if it no longer holds a significant place in many universities and colleges, we can at least be aware of the host of books still in print with similar scope. Some of these are cited throughout the book. To an extent, then, the summary offered here may be treated a kind of primer to aid one's own search for our relevant historic milestones.

For the sake of convenience, the fifteen chapters of the book can be viewed in somewhat distinctive clusters. Chapters One, Two and Three—the three *Rs* of Rousseau, Revolution, and Reaction—are grounded in the last decades of the eighteenth century, the height of the Enlightenment. These chapters flow together as a frame for discussing the concept of *authority*—who has it and why; how is it being exercised; and what changes are warranted.

The challenge for thinkers like Jean Jacques Rousseau was, first, to account for the experience of domination that was characteristic of the fading feudalism of his age, emulated in other institutions including the elites of the church and crown. Secondly, Rousseau sought to challenge the traditional view that man was essentially selfish and could not, without such hierarchies of power, be forced to live together in peace. Rousseau thought that human beings are not naturally purely self-centered, but are, rather, capable of cooperation with each other as we become aware of the range of vulnerabilities we have in common. The recognition of such features of life — scarcity, disease, or the lessened capacity of old age — allows us to reflect the spirit of compassion just as inherent in us as the equally powerful instinct to preserve our own lives and promote our wellbeing.

The title of Chapter One, "Emile's Tutor/Our Guide," invites attention to Rousseau's insistence that achieving a more egalitarian society cannot succeed without working out how to educate our children. Through the lens of Rousseau's most widely-read book, *Emile*, we see how he pairs our design of education with constant regard for nature's instructive presence in the wider world beyond the institutional contrivances our social history has bequeathed us.

Chapter Two chronicles two revolutions, 1776 and 1789, mainly by establishing their connection to the ideas of Rousseau's generation and by parsing the two iconic documents associated with them: The Declaration of Independence in America's case; and the Declaration of the Rights of Man and Citizen for the French. Both have left large footprints in political thought and continue to be mined by scholars and reformers around the world. Even though Rousseau did not live to see the French Revolution, nor did he espouse armed revolt for political reform, the French posthumously honored him on the very first anniversary of the fall of the Bastille as if he had been one of its leaders. The characters of the two revolutions are contrasted—one said to be for *independence*—aka regime change, the other an avowed assault on existing social and legal traditions. Implications from each and the formative declarations they produced, find expression in many subsequent eras covered in this book. Both documents reflect, albeit with differing emphases and scope, the essential equality of human beings as bearers of rights to be protected by government based on consent of the governed.

"Reaction," the subject of Chapter Three, recounts how some observers responded to the French Revolution posing a threat to the stability of institutions worthy of retention, such as a constitutional monarchy. Edmund Burke in Britain thus condemned what the French had done—although initially they did not aim to depose their king—not so much for their sake as for his fear of what some in Britain were writing and speaking of at the time. One of them, fellow British writer Mary Wollstonecraft, took up the pen to applaud what the French had done. Her concerns went beyond the monarchy as she called for wide access for the right to vote in parliamentary elections, and for reform of laws subordinating women in civil society.

The character of reaction is not simply a reflexive opposition to change. It comes in varying shades. For instance, a near contemporary of Edmund Burke, Alexis de Tocqueville of France, saw the prospect of greater equality as the main force of change from feudalism to a more liberal social order, not just for France but for all European countries and those influenced by them, like the United States. Tocqueville, however, worried about a lowering of standards of taste in the arts and beyond, a coarsening, of what makes up the social order he was used to, even the bourgeois part of that order. That's what he would miss in the demise of the nobility—*noblesse oblige*. Seen in its largest light, we might see Tocqueville's worry as a fear that education would not accomplish what Emile's tutor had in mind—responsible citizenship that requires building our capacity to moderate our own individual appetites. A person's character, not reason alone, will determine the quality of social life in a world of greater equality.

Chapter Four, the "Juggernaut of Commerce," takes our account well into the nineteenth century and into that distinctive era and mindset historians have named the Industrial Revolution. It is the time of growth of factories and a shift of rural folk into cities to work in them. There is, to be sure, an increase thereby in liberty of movement but precious little equalizing of incomes or job security. Memorable figures in literature like Charles Dickens have given us vivid scenes of the plight of the urban poor in the England of Victoria's time. Others took to the tasks of addressing some of these issues directly. Our exemplar is an unlikely reformer or philanthropist, a mill owner in Scotland named Robert Owen. His gift to the story of material challenges to equality that accompanied the new wealth of the Atlantic world was an idea not explicitly political. Owen sought to demonstrate that small communities of working families could sustain themselves through cooperative associations and share amenities like education for children and adults. Like Rousseau, he believed that institutions could serve communities of equality without hierarchy or exploitation.

The fact that Owen's first experimental community in Scotland was based around textile mills illustrates two things about this era. One was that mass production of anything requires not only capital but also a ready labor supply. Textiles as an industry became virtually synonymous with the material improvements of nineteenth-century Britain. The principal resource involved was cotton—much less expensive to turn into a fabric than either linen or wool. It became the default clothing material of working folk everywhere.

A singular irony about this period is that it produced an unprecedented international effort to confront the harshest legacy of imperialism and colonialism, the Atlantic slave trade. Moved by the consciences of notable Quakers like William Wilberforce, the effort was mounted for Parliament to weigh in, and it did. The importance of this extraordinary initiative is seen again in the later chapter on the abolition of lawful slavery in the United States.

By the time the experiments in the cooperative communities of Robert Owen had inspired the creation of workers unions, new insights and concerns among political theorists emerged, too. They are represented in Chapter Five's focus on John Stuart Mill and Herbert Spencer. Material conditions changed enough to produce a middle class and these in turn produced greater voter participation in government. Nonetheless Mill was concerned that a new dominance could emerge and produce a "tyranny of the majority" just as threatening as the old order of oligarchy. His worries led to the writing of *On Liberty*, whose influence has been and continues to be considerable. The idea of individualism that Mill advanced did not curtail the equality in basic rights or suggest that government should not try to ameliorate conditions of economic inequality. No, Herbert Spencer adopted that stance. His concern was that if we collectively tried too hard to promote equality, we might interfere with nature's evolution of the competitive spirit that Darwin's new science claimed. The tension between these two sets of ideas reflects an ongoing—and at least latent—division in political thought and policy of the present century. Broadly, the tension revealed from Mill and Spencer's thinking, though not always acknowledged as such, remains in the split between "liberal" and "conservative" or "libertarian," opinion on many issues, especially with regard to economics.

The next four chapters—Six, Seven, Eight, and Nine—relate to each other across both the new economic divide prevalent in Western societies, but also via the more basic but lingering question of racial subjugation in American slavery. The latter problem comes to a head in the Civil War under President Lincoln, yet major thinkers had been greatly troubled about it for some time, as suggested in Chapter Four. Both J.S. Mill and Herbert Spencer were appalled by slavery, as was another stalwart of individualism introduced in Chapter Five—Ralph Waldo Emerson. Major leaders of the abolition movement like Frederick Douglass and William Lloyd Garrison are identified and followed. The policy highlights of Chapter Six include the Thirteenth, Fourteenth, and Fifteenth Amendments to the Constitution of the United States, marking a profound extension of individual rights from those contained in the original.

Chapter Seven's treatment of Reconstruction, both its initial prospects as well as its ultimate failure, is seen through the scholarship of W.E.B. Dubois and Eric Foner. That experiment's failure shaded the record of what did and did not happen, as commercial exploitation in newly settled parts of the Midwest took hold.

New partisan alliances reflected the formation of a new consciousness. Populists and then Progressives drew to some extent on the shifting and uncertain identities of traditional Republican and Democratic parties. Progressives finally found their voice in such innovations as Jane Addams's Hull House, serving the urban poor by community building at the neighborhood level. President Theodore Roosevelt became the face of the Progressives' confrontation with an important aspect of economic growth—the size and power of corporations athwart many banks, railroads and oil companies. He applied anti-trust laws with vigor. And taxes, both income and estate, transitioned into more than mere wartime expedients. Important scholarship reflected in these several chapters include works by Daniel T. Rodgers, *Atlantic Crossings, Social Politics in a Progressive Age* (1998), Michael McGerr, *A Fierce Discontent—The Rise and Fall the Progressive Movement in America, 1870–1920* (2003), and Jill Lapore, *These Truths, a History of the United States* (2018).

"The Citizenship of Women," Chapter Ten, owes its relatively late place in the chronology of this book to the anachronism of its maturing, formally, only in the twentieth century. The national adoption of the right to vote for some women might well have arrived a century earlier, when America caught up with the ideals of its founding document and made former slaves voting members of our national community. Or it might just as easily have come when the French proclaimed universal rights for all people, in 1789, and managed shortly thereafter to legislate an end to slavery in French colonial territory. But women were put off then, too, and did not surface as a national concern until around the time of America's own advance more than a century later.

Those women who ultimately prevailed in the effort would have little doubt that the power exercised by men, and only by men, was the barrier they needed to confront, not merely in writing but in organizations formed for the purpose. Hearty souls like Elizabeth Cady Stanton, Lucretia Mott, and Susan B. Anthony, who as early as 1848 assembled the first women's political conclave in upstate New York, the Seneca Conference, launched a movement—the missing piece for success. They certainly were aware of and took heart from the writings of Mary Wollstonecraft's 1792 book, *A Vindication of the Rights of Women*. It also helped that in 1869 noted British philosopher J.S. Mill published, with the aid of his wife Harriet Taylor, his book *The Subjection of Women*. Disappointments occurred along the course of bringing about the Nineteenth Amendment, none more telling than abolitionists like Frederick Douglass who declined to support the inclusion of women with adoption of the Fifteenth Amendment (extending the right to vote to former slaves) by Congress after the Civil War. The broad depth and scope of this women's movement is chronicled by twentieth century scholar Christine Stansell in *The Feminist Promise, 1792 to the Present* (2010).

Three periods of national and international crisis occupy the foreground of Chapters Eleven, Twelve, and Thirteen: the Great Depression of the 1930s; World War II and restoration initiatives afterward; and finally the Cold War at home and abroad. The stock market crash of 1929 and the ensuing flattening of demand in the economy left millions of Americans unemployed. The challenges for the new national administration of the Democrats under President Franklin Roosevelt in 1932 demanded creative solutions.

Perhaps the New Deal is most popularly remembered for the bold new agencies designed to put people back to work, such as the Public Works Administration and the Civilian Conservation Corps. Even more enduring, though, was the program known as Social Security designed to provide assistance to those without work and safeguard those most vulnerable to aging or disability, whether related directly to the Depression or not. The innovation seemed radical for an America that had not long before lived through an era of marked economic expansion but social indifference, known as the Gilded Age, in the late 1800s and early 1900s. Perhaps the ultimate political persuaders of this pervasive change in the country's fortunes gripping the American electorate of 1932 rested in human fear and social anxiety. The very title of an important history of the period points in this direction: *Freedom from Fear: The American People in Depression and War, 1929–1945* by David M. Kennedy (1999).

The recognition of pervasive human need warrants the central place in the memories of those who lived through that time or were reliably informed about in the next generation. The broader and more basic initiatives launched by FDR's New Deal in the 1930s maintained a simple free market system. The creation of an agency to regulate the stock market—the Securities Exchange Commission (SEC), and another to insure some public oversight of the cost of credit—the Federal Reserve, demonstrate that the New Deal had systemic adjustments in mind when it spawned the "back to work" stimulus agencies, most of them meant only for temporary existence.

Between these two sets of policies and programs, another looks more directly at dislocations caused by a market economy grown ever more complex since the time of Chapter Four's Robert Owen and the nascent years of the Industrial Revolution. It insured—or made more likely—that workers could gain more job security, compensation, and tolerable work conditions. The creation of a National Labor Relations Board to oversee disputes in industry between management and labor—made stronger by a federal guarantee of collective bargaining—notably engendered a rise in union membership after the passage of the Wagner Act of 1935. The Fair Labor Standards Act of 1938 added the limitation of a forty-hour work week and imposed a minimum wage. But the statute excluded agricultural and domestic service workers from its benefits, limitations that over the decades since then only increased the disparity of incomes of Blacks and immigrants from national averages.

Chapter Twelve, "Domestic Innovation and New International Cooperation Following World War II," demonstrates how a nation with one big crisis—the Great Depression—already confronted, if not controlled—in imaginative, pragmatic ways, can shift its focus and fight a war across two oceans simultaneously. Mobilization—a frequently used characterization on the home front—meant many more factories making a host of instruments of war, but it also meant, especially significant for themes of this book, a greatly expanded work force. Much of that expansion included women going to work in the defense industries of the 1940s for the first time. Traditional roles for women gave way to a new kind of consciousness touched by egalitarianism. To an extent this was also true of men in uniform. Drawn from the full range of social-economic backgrounds and regions, soldiers and sailors could find comradery—not to mention disciplined cooperation—across boundaries from civilian life.

Yet at least one of those barriers was nonetheless carried into the army. Units of soldiers were segregated by race, a carryover from civilian life for many and not changed until President Harry Truman in 1948 issued an exec-utive order ending segregation in the armed forces.

Aware of the many lives disrupted by the war, Congress, in 1944, enacted the Compensatory Service Act, commonly known as the G.I. Bill, providing a number of financial benefits for veterans. The educational part of the benefits—the big national investment—was on a par at least with the Land-Grant College program under the Morrill Act of the Lincoln presidency.

Of the many post-war social and political adjustments experienced by allies of the United States, none was more striking than that of Great Britain. They changed their government in ways that reflected not merely a shift of leading political parties but a more egalitarian outlook in much of the popu-lation, having been challenged by a desperate war effort. Among other major innovations, Britain created a National Health Service, which remains the singular feature of the post-war foundation of a welfare state. Angus Calder, in *The People's War, Britain 1929–45* (1969), identifies causative factors leading to the changes and backgrounds of the then-new leadership of Britain.

Perhaps not surprising, worldwide war resulted in important develop-ments beyond those in domestic society. The cast of international relations changed decisively as well, in more sweeping and enduring ways than the period following World War I. Led by the United States, the United Nations was created almost as soon as the war had ended, its objectives not limited to future peace keeping but extended most immediately to relief from the mate-rial destruction and human dislocation caused by the war. UNRRA, United Nations Relief and Rehabilitation Agency, represented the first thrust of this kind of cooperation, which in turn led to other, more specialized agencies like the International Refugee Administration and the World Health Orga-nization.

Mary Ann Glendon captures the spirit of the age, and America's role in its innovations are captured in her book, *A World Made New: Eleanor Roosevelt and the Universal Declaration of Human Rights* (2002), about the 1948 treaty that adopted and published the first global statement of consensus on human rights. The resemblance to and inspiration from revolutionary documents like the French Declaration of the Rights of Man and Citizen of 1789 and the American Declaration of Independence of 1776 are unmistakable.

In a way the Cold War, discussed in Chapter Thirteen, is more than metaphorical, for during the 1960s there were armed conflicts in one place or another in the world. Most of them, however, involved surrogates of the larger powers who could, but were unwilling to, engage in something approximating a World War III. The atmosphere, however, between the Soviet Union and the United States—one of mutual suspicion and latent hostility—had its counterpart within American politics. The pejorative term McCarthyism, for example, still recognized and employed, implies an aspect of the widespread reaction to hints of subversion or disloyalty by alleged agents or fellow travelers of communism.

There is a distinctive irony here. While the international dimension of the 1960s looked in one direction—ideological systems locked in a dangerous competition about their separate value and legitimacy—the experience of our domestic social and political challenge played out in a different one. Thus, the two main figures in this account developed a sort of complementary set of initiatives producing both advances in civil rights legislation and a new recognition of the pervasiveness of economic inequality.

Both Dr. Martin Luther King, Jr., and President Lyndon Johnson played distinctive roles, but the convergence of their efforts produced what Dr. Rev. William J. Barber II has called a "second Reconstruction," in his 2016 book, *The Third Reconstruction: How A Moral Movement is Overcoming The Politics of Division and Fear*. He refers to the several Civil Rights acts of the Johnson years, 1964, 1965 and 1968, that together insured greater federal protection for voting rights of minorities, long challenged by poll taxes and literacy tests in states of the South. By most accounts, these legislative breakthroughs would not have happened when they did but for the protest movement driven by the disciplined passion and genius of Dr. Martin L. King, Jr.

Less widely appreciated, perhaps, are the advances generated through Johnson's Great Society initiatives to challenge poverty through neighborhood and community development under the Office of Economic Opportunity. Two initiatives went beyond what FDR's New Deal did in similar areas; one freed work places from discrimination in hiring or on-the-job treatment, the Equal Employment Opportunity Commission, and the other dramatically expanded Social Security by creating Medicare for all seniors 65 or older.

Finally, the fact that federal taxes remained about where they were after World War II meant the impact of those taxes sharply reduced the disparities of wealth and income that prevailed before the Great Depression. Economist Richard Pomfret reflects on this in his 2011 book *The Age of Equality: The Twentieth Century in Economic Perspective.*

Chapter Fourteen, "Philosophy Needs History," explicitly examines two broad assessments regarding how philosophy and history are interwoven. One position maintains that so much of the theoretical work done in the preceding two hundred years plus proceeded as if the ideals could and/or should have universal application, for any age, in any country—an assumption explicit in the French 1789 Declaration of the Rights of Man and Citizen, and strongly implied in the opening paragraph of America's Declaration of Independence.

A separate answer addresses twentieth-century philosophical scholarship typically written in abstract terms and not tied to the issues of particular times or circumstances. John Rawls gave us an example in *A Theory of Justice* (1973). He famously worked out imaginative—deliberately identified as heuristic—devices, like the veil of ignorance. His work, for a time, prompted reconsideration of the venerable concept of the Social Contract last treated seriously by John Stuart Mill nearly one hundred years earlier.

A major rejoinder to Rawls was written by Robert Nozick— *Anarchy, State and Utopia* (1974)—in which he claimed that any "re-distributive" public policies (part of Rawls's formula would target the least advantaged members of society) would have first to establish that existing distributions are themselves unjust or illegitimate.[5]

Later twentieth-century scholarship from philosophers has tried to untie contemporary critiques of inequality or proposals for greater equality from the two imperfections just mentioned. The ones this chapter relied on do not try to define equality as an abstract ideal.[6] Rather, they try to relate our understandings of the term to particular initiatives or issues of some urgency in particular societies, like the United States, in existing circumstances. Michael Walzer in his 1983 book *Spheres of Justice: A Defense of Pluralism and Equality* calls this another way of doing philosophy—namely by using history to interpret the shared meanings our country has given to relations or distributions in the past.

This approach leads Walzer to present a working definition for these purposes so as to comprehend a society of equals as one in which no one or

---

[5] Bernard Williams explores Nozick's idea in *The Moral View of Politics: Essays and Reviews, 1959-2002,* (Princeton: Princeton University Press, 2014), 122.

[6] *Equality of what?* is the challenge of modern economist Amartya Sen, author of *Inequality Re-examined* (1995). Attempts to answer have fallen into three broad categories: *basic* (or political-legal as in a citizen's equality before the law); *economic* as in equal pay for equal work; and *relational* as in mutual respect among individuals.

no group has the power to dominate others in respect of any of the complex of social goods that we see operative already. In other words, the concept of living as equals is negative in character, much as liberty is often defined in terms of freedom *from* oppression or other deprivation such as in speech, assembly, or belief.

In what other respects are liberty and equality similar and why does it matter? Is one more the province of official or state action? The title of this book implies that both ideals form part of a common reality, part social and part political. If that is true, how might we best understand the connections between the "social" or "material" realm of life and the political part? Where or how might we find those links?

More specifically, our book title implies more than a casual or random tie. Liberty indeed is cast as the family member from whom equality is *lost*. A related implication might be that both ideals are important enough under our existing forms and traditions of government that they should be pursued or supported together. It is often claimed, on the other hand, that the advance of one undermines the other—that the more equal our society becomes, at least in economic terms, the less liberty there is. How might we test or appraise that claim?

Chapter One: How Rousseau Became Our Guide

In the course of showing how mankind had built a social prison for itself, Rousseau produced a veritable encyclopedia of egalitarian ideas, unique both in its scope and in the personal passion that informs it...He did not invent the secular idea of equality, but he was its most complete and eloquent defender...When he announced to his shocked readers that all our vices had their origins in inequality, he meant to take a wholly new view of the moral world: the way it looks from the very bottom of society.[7]

In assembling a gallery of equality's heroes, we might begin with the English barons at Runnymede. They confronted the absolutist tendencies of King John in 1215 and came away with the Magna Carta as a critical milestone in the evolution of political and legal rights. Or we might look at the revolutionary German cleric, Martin Luther, and his dramatic assault on the hierarchy of Christian faith in the 1400s; or, just as easily, the Levelers of England in the 1600s with their opposition to distinctions of material wealth. And while all of these men have made important contributions to our store of experience with inequality and injustice, we must recognize that despite not having risked life or limb, Jean-Jacques Rousseau may have best understood the character of equality. Since he first published his controversial *Discourse on the Arts and Sciences* in 1750, his writing—reinforced with passionate convictions based on personal experience and direct observation—has influenced substantial thinkers for centuries.

---

[7] Judith N. Shklar, "Rousseau for Our Time," *Daedalus*, 170 No. 3, (Summer 1978), 11.

A quasi member of the French *philosophes*, he sparred often with Voltaire and a young Denis Diderot, men who share the same spot in history, but with very different views regarding society. Rousseau only partially subscribed to the primacy of human reasoning, one of the lodestars of the Enlightenment. He did not discount a role for the emotions nor disqualify traditions—like the primacy of the family as the basic social unit—from playing into his systematic thinking. Did he believe in human progress? Not particularly. And while he did not expect science alone could insure it, he did think that science could teach us better to understand the natural world. Human beings in society must struggle both within themselves and with each other to reach a degree of happiness and freedom unknown up to and including his own time. And therein lies Rousseau's special resonance for Western thought through to the twenty-first century.

With so many wars, excesses of barbarism, collapses of regimes and empires, not to mention the racial and sectarian enmity and environmental degradation in the two-plus centuries between Rousseau and ourselves, we may find it hard to remain optimistic about the future of mankind or civilization. Why do we keep trying "to get it right"? Can we afford to do otherwise?

In simplest terms, Rousseau would champion the strength of our feelings of empathy and compassion for each other regardless of any imbalance in our political or societal harmony. However, the institutional arrangements we have inherited—or helped create—and tolerate, thwart any feelings of shared identity with others. Such is the case when people of great wealth lord it over those beholden to them for a place in society, for a job or position. Such is also the case when individuals, thus in inferior positions, seek some special connection to those in authority and in turn betray their fellow servants with slights or scheming.

Dramas like the twentieth-century *Upstairs Downstairs* and twenty-first century *Downton Abbey* turn on such dynamics. Dynamics that Judith Shklar notes, in her *Daedalus* essay "Jean-Jacques Rousseau and Equality," influenced an impressionable Jean-Jacques, who, as "a footman in several households...could speak of this peculiarly degrading situation as an insider. It was here that he learned to hate violently the ruling classes whose cruelty, pettiness, prejudices and vices revolted him to the end of his days."[8]

No radical, however much his critics have miscast him, Rousseau did not endorse a program of revolution by actual force of arms. He trusted the sentiments of ordinary people and considered himself one of them, even after

---

[8] Shklar, "Rousseau for Our Time," 11.

obtaining fame as a writer. He despised the condescension of France's establishment and even the conceits of men like himself who eked out a living by sculpting, painting or writing poetry, prose or music in the garrets of Paris.

Distinguishing people for their words or other arts sat no better with him than pride in holding a great estate or title. He mistrusted the theater for the same reason—perhaps his biggest bone of contention with Voltaire. He saw people affecting poses, whether to amuse for the moment or invite attention to contemporary manners, as nothing more than a ruse to mislead and corrupt the audience. Does this reflect his Geneva birth and childhood, his Calvinist rearing? Of course. Does it still have relevance to us? Consider how the twenty-first century entertainment industry—theater writ large—and its pervasive and, some say, insidious nature captures so much of our attention and adulation, underscoring his point.

Rousseau did not make up his mind to be somebody. He went about learning what the world had to teach him, serving as a domestic servant, personal tutor, and secretary to important people like the French ambassador to Venice. His continuing association and correspondence with significant people in Geneva gave him real problems, political and cultural, to think about, and gave birth to many of his ideas and major works. We might even call him an itinerant opportunist who embraced extensions of good fortune where he could find them.

The Calvinist religious tradition of Geneva had, by his time, become less about church doctrine and more about ethics. That did not mean, however, that pious supporters were any less vocal and provocative about politics and society. The question of the theater, a hot-button cultural issue of the day, found Rousseau differing from other leading voices of the Enlightenment. Officially, the city banned the production of plays in public, but a private lively theater scene thrived in the homes and salons of Geneva. Some of the plays came from Paris, including those of Voltaire until he left Geneva for the friendlier atmosphere of Lausanne.

As Helena Rosenblatt claims in *Rousseau and Geneva*, Rousseau's views offered the ordinary pastors of Geneva a modicum of encouragement vis-à-vis the wealthy magistrates of the city who privately opposed the ban but gave grudging lip service to it. The clergy could, with the blessings of a Rousseau, speak more authoritatively to their congregations without feeling the quiet pressure from the upper crust to change their tune or remain silent. At the same time, Rousseau argued that public theater in a city Geneva's size would inevitably involve a tax, one that would affect lower income citizens more than the affluent. He considered such a tax regressive, much the way modern-day Americans see sales tax.

His views however, did not keep him from participating in the arts. His passion for music spilled into mathematics. And while the innovative musical notation system that he devised did not meet with the standards of acceptance to the Académie des Sciences, he used it to compose his first opera, *Les Muses Galantes*. His first big break, though, came through an essay contest sponsored by the Académie de Dijon that asked entrants to discuss whether the arts and sciences had been beneficial to the development of morality.

Rousseau's categorical "no" in his essay, *Discourse on the Arts and Sciences*, won him the contest and he quickly gained recognition—good and bad—from its publication. He maintained that art and science, so far, had merely bestowed greater marks of distinction among human beings, thereby corrupting them into striving for advantage over others. While science holds the promise of making their livelihoods less grinding and degrading, he argued, the most obvious impact instead provides individuals with greater material or social leverage and does not better the lives of ordinary people.

In his subsequent essay, *Discourse on the Origins of Inequality*, he extends his indictment from the arts and sciences to political traditions. Rousseau posits that man in nature, while free, has only a tacit recognition of the existential need for cooperation that has so far only betrayed him into conditions of either superiority or inferiority, and mutual dependency, but not mutual respect. The earliest villain in human social history, for Rousseau, likely was the first person who, after tilling some space of land, built a fence around it and declared, "This is mine." Thus, the very presence of the ancient institution of property became an anathema to our capacity for sharing.

Despite the inspiration he drew from the simple beauty of the Swiss, French, and Italian landscapes, he did not advocate for a utopian return to the state of nature, believing that we cannot return to a supposed golden age of humankind's earliest existence. He professed a lifelong quest for personal reform but did not necessarily seek to design particular changes in government. He fundamentally mistrusted our collective capacity for institutionalizing our mutual dependency—something we must square with the innocent self-love men have from birth. Yet, he went on to write at length about the construct of a real or supposed state of nature preceding our common efforts to construct serviceable social institutions.

The usefulness and influence of social contract theory has continuously influenced humankind since the days of Socrates, in part because it contains a central justification for government of any stripe—liberal or conservative.

In return for our allegiance to the state, the state, in turn, promises security of person and property. In the seventeenth century, Thomas Hobbes delivered an exhaustive inquiry of the issue in his 1651 tome, *Leviathan*. Nearly forty years later, John Locke, considered the Father of Liberalism, furthered the discussion in his 1689 *Two Treatises of Government*. Building on their observations, Rousseau, in his 1782 *The Social Contract*, addresses the construct of state of nature—real or supposed—that precedes our common efforts to construct serviceable social institutions.

Hobbes's version of the social contract presupposes that humans have a largely selfish and fearful nature, and therefore they require a Leviathan or strong central leader to establish obedience as the quid pro quo for the security of society members at large. Locke, on the other hand, assumed a gentler model of human nature and believed that we have the capacity for cooperation with each other to foster the common good. Only partly selfish, humans can also empathize and see their own good served by seeing to the interests of others. In the political world that requires more of a citizen than mere allegiance to a sovereign; each citizen must participate in the process by selecting leaders—a government—to oversee society.

Rousseau, however, wanted us to consider the contradiction between the obvious need for mutual cooperation in daily life with our historic tendency to corrupt that need. He insists that a credible model of social contract must account for our morality. Do we have the capacity to limit our own appetites under any circumstances? He qualifies his answer with a commitment to respect every other member of society enough to see every member as part of the overall sovereignty of self-government. Leaders must simply administer the laws adopted by the membership; leadership—whether selected, invited, or even inherited—has to remain faithful to the laws established by the people. Rousseau thus coins a third version of the social contract: we commit our allegiance not to any sort of leader, maximum or minimum, but to each other.

More often criticized or misunderstood than any other, his most original political idea maintains that the state, or a government, only has authority— can only rule with legitimacy—if it does so in accordance with what he termed the general will of the people. His contemporaries understood it as a call for laws approved by people at large. Since that time, historians and philosophers have yet to determine a form of government fit to deliver on that idea. Moreover, not a few critical readers of Rousseau's work have suggested his idea of a general will presages a state of totalitarian character, like Fascism or Communism, perhaps pointing to his oft-cited proposition that "people must be forced to be free."

Richard Dagger, in *Civic Virtues*, explains that Rousseau invokes *moral* freedom, not natural freedom or civic freedom. The citizens, under their social contract, have the choice to either violate the law, which they, as part of the sovereign whole of the people, approved, or change their minds and comply. If more than a few such free-riders choose the former, then, yes, they will undermine the efficacy of the political order.

Rousseau implies that through the General Will, a degree of equality will be achieved. And that it will be sufficient to prevent distortion by too much or too little wealth for any particular member: no one has enough money to "buy" the dependence of another, nor does anyone have so little money that they must "sell" themselves for their livelihood. Freedom, therefore, depends upon the premise of this legitimate moral equality under such a social contract, for it upholds the very cooperative practices essential to it.

Rousseau did not endorse a system of representative democracy. He might, like Plato, just as readily favor an oligarchy of talented individuals. Indeed, he does not rule out a monarchy as long as the ruler remains faithful to the general will. He does not strive for mere majority rule but for a greater depth of equality so intrinsically linked to liberty that they will advance together or falter in comparable measure.

Hence the enduring significance of the general will. Generation after generation, we must continue to craft our proposed laws and policies in a way that everyone agrees will benefit each of us. Some laws might more directly affect some, more indirectly others—as with, for example, variable rates of taxation—but *in toto* they should serve us all. Not merely the majority of us. All of us. Some pay more, some less, but everyone benefits from the social goods—such as roads, bridges and schools—shared throughout society. By seeing each other as equals, we will in fact find ourselves freer than if we merely sought to advance our own individual interests as competitors. Not only do we reduce scarcity, but we enhance mutual empathy.

Rousseau calls for us to suspend our ideological bents, and even our awareness of our individual special gifts or needs, and think of society as a whole. In 1785, an intrigued Immanuel Kant published his "Categorical Imperative" in which he declares that moral human action must pass the test of universal application. Similarly, almost two hundred years later, philosopher John Rawls, following the intellectual tradition of the social contract, constructed his heuristic device of the Original Position on Rousseau.

In his 1971 book, *A Theory of Justice*, Rawls explicitly asks his readers—and through them, those in positions of public authority—to engage in a thought experiment. Imagine that you do not know, as a human being, what individual capacities or talents or fortuities of wealth you will possess, and thus you do not know what kind of policies you might likely choose from behind that "veil of ignorance."[9] Rawls suggests we would likely vote in favor of a system of distributive justice different from the one we would enact if we in fact knew these things about ourselves—about our place in the world—as we vote. Unlike Rousseau and Kant, Rawls speaks to the reality of great divisions in modern societies based on a wide range of differences including race, religion, gender, ethnicity, age, and of course socio-economic standing.

While Locke sees natural rights as the expression of divine endowment in human reason, Rousseau engages the realm of nature very differently, less metaphysically. Nature can remind us that but for the growth and perpetuation of traditional institutions of hierarchies and layers of power and prestige—the old stuff of our civilization, we can learn to live as equals if we consciously acknowledge each other's vulnerabilities. Nature, in short, reminds us what we are, but it cannot ordain what we do or how we should proceed to live together in peace.

Emile began as a treatise on education and grew into what would become Rousseau's most widely read book. In it, he addresses the intersection of the state of nature and the social contract.[10] He traces the interaction between a self-modeled tutor and his pupil from childhood through the stages of his intellectual and moral development. Starting from an understanding common to other writers about the state of nature and the social contract—namely that we are born with an instinct for self-preservation—he parts company with them soon after. He does not believe that the individual human being will necessarily become fearful of others or envious of their greater strengths or assets—we can grow self-regard into a social cohesion not based on coercion, intimidation or resignation. Society need not turn people into a jealous and fearful citizenry (although historically it has done that). It can instead become the common ground of recognizing unique individuals joined by cooperation with and mutual empathy for others.

---

[9] John Rawls, *A Theory of Justice*, (Cambridge: Harvard University Press, 1971).

[10] Recent scholarship reveals that the incentive for the book came from his readers' reaction to the "desolate description of French society" in the earlier works sketched above. Philosopher Susan Neiman claims that Rousseau published *Emile* as a proposed "remedy for the sickness of civilization." Susan Neiman, *Moral Clarity: A Guide for Grown-Up Idealists*, (Princeton: Princeton University Press, 2009) 259.

Rousseau knows from personal experience that developing a feel for cooperation and empathy best comes from learning by example, not by didactic instruction. He believed in encouraging children to follow their curiosity about the natural world around them and to understand that the forces of nature have to do with necessity and not will power; to avoid the traditional hierarchical family and village life contests of will. For example, early on, Emile reads *Robinson Crusoe* to see how the title character learns to survive on his expanding acquaintance with his natural surroundings. When it comes to the more advanced reading of the classics, Rousseau draws on his own early reading of Herodotus that highlighted the blights of vanity and vainglory often exhibited by great men, and he has the tutor encourage Emile to see the heroes as mortals rather than gods on an elevated plane beyond his comprehension.

This pedagogy preserves the individual's sense of worth by encouraging growth without introducing the socially destructive vices of envy or resentment, or the overweening place of pride that has crept into our cooperation with others in various kinds of social associations. Rousseau blames those attitudes for the inequality and instability in our institutions, especially regarding educational elitism, and social and professional nepotism and cronyism. Rather than seeing others as strivers and achievers, Emile's education allows him to understand that everyone suffers in some way. It helps him develop empathy and compassion which, when left to themselves, become just as powerful as self-interest. *Emile* illustrates how Rousseau, as Allan Bloom suggests, has done for the "soul of man what Montesquieu did for our government in inventing the separation and balance of powers." Compassion drawn from the sense of human equality becomes the "glue binding men together" and not sheer self-interest.[11]

Rousseau has given us, has imbued in more than two centuries of subsequent thought, three principles borne of observation: the intrinsic link between freedom and equality; the immutability of what he introduced as general will; and the importance of education—three things we will return to throughout this discussion.

---

[11] Allan Bloom, "The Education of Democratic Man: *Emile*," *Daedalus*, 107, No. 3, (Summer 1978), 135, 150.

Chapter Two: Revolution

Enlightenment's Reach

Allan Bloom's mention of one of Rousseau's notable contemporaries, Baron de la Brède et de Montesquieu (1689–1755), illustrates how far the ideas of that special time have traveled and how deeply they have influenced us.[12] Understanding his influence on some of the founders of the American republic promises a more critical view of our traditions and interpretations of historic documents like the Constitution and its structures of government.

The very notion of an "Age of Enlightenment" derives from the creative energies of a score or so of men and a handful of women, most of them privileged, who in the eighteenth century formed a critical mass of thinking, reflection, imagination—and, most importantly, writing—that gave intellectual form to the Modern Age. Each one of these writers left something of value, especially when our focus turns to particular social-political ideas like liberty and equality.

Britain had David Hume, Francis Hutcheson and Adam Smith, America had Benjamin Franklin and Thomas Jefferson, and Germany Immanuel Kant. But the ones who belong with Rousseau in the subset of those thinking seriously at the time about equality lived in France: Condorcet, Diderot, Helvetius, Holbach, and Voltaire. For example, Denis Diderot, a true contemporary of Rousseau's, anticipated his colleague's version of the social contract in arguing for a reconciliation of reason and feeling lest there continue to be detrimental effects on virtue. He edited the first collective, comprehensive

---

[12] Allan Bloom edited the 1947 Everyman Classics edition of *Emile*.

compilation of man's knowledge of the world. As a deist, his views led to conflict with the Church during his seniority.

Most certainly the overarching name that best encompasses the Enlightenment project was and is Voltaire (*né*: François-Marie Arouet, 1694–1778). His stature has more to do with his continuing fight for independent inquiry and exposition than for systematic thinking about the nature of society or political philosophy on a grand scale. More libertarian than egalitarian, he favored leadership by those best fit to exercise its requirements. The central place of reason and tolerance in Enlightenment thought is as thoroughly burnished as it is thanks in no small measure to his writing and to his activism through much of his long life. While probably deliberately obscure about his ties to religion, he made no secret of his disdain for clerical authority and dogma. Voltaire was clearly de facto leader of the group history knows as the *philosophes*. Their bond found practical strength through work on the world's earliest multi-volume compendium of knowledge, *L'Encyclopédie*, an endeavor filled with the promise of science and reason unfettered by speculation or superstition. Work on its English cousin the *Britannica* began a decade later.

America's Conflict with Great Britain

It was slow in coming. As Julie Flavell points out in *When London Was Capital of America*, the several million European migrants and their kin who made their home on the western shores of the North Atlantic in the 1770s did not think of themselves as separate from the British Empire. While they tied most of their civic identities to a particular colony, from Massachusetts Bay to Georgia, for a hundred years they recognized that their ultimate political direction came from London. Many, if not most, found the relationship a positive one. The standard of living, for example, of the average New England family was higher than that of the average English one. Moreover, personal freedoms like that of religious affiliation were better protected in many, if not all, of the colonies. As Bernard Bailyn describes in *The Ideological Origins of the American Revolution*, the variety of official or tacit tolerance of religious difference extended from the most liberal in Pennsylvania, where the Quakers settled, to the most conservative southern colonies of Virginia and the Carolinas, where the Church of England remained the official denomination. The New England colonies fell somewhere in between, with divergencies by sect the norm.

So, why was there a revolution in America? Bailyn goes on to argue that the pamphlets, articles, and sermons throughout the 1700s highlighted the impact of British disputes from the previous century, like Puritanism and challenges to royal authority. This literature reveals a more enduring influence in the colonies than in England itself. Because these ideas were still in circulation, current imperial pressure forced them to the surface, and the call for liberty gained momentum. These ideas became the background, the context of, if not the driving force for, America's challenge to Britain.

Why was there any reason for change? The short answer is that the imperial needs of the mother country took precedence and forced issues that might have lingered longer. The French and Indian War, 1754–1763, was expensive for Great Britain. London believed it only fair that Americans should help pay the debt and attempted to levy various taxes, which colonists, in turn, resisted. In the spring of 1775, just a year after the tax on tea led to a protest in Boston Harbor, the push back against things like quartering troops in local homes and suspending trials by jury finally produced the exchange of rifle shots in the quiet towns of Concord and Lexington.

The colonials managed to meet in Philadelphia by the summer of 1776, establishing a collaboration among neighboring communities not witnessed since Benjamin Franklin's 1759 unsuccessful attempt to form a compact of colonies in Albany, New York. The Philadelphia Convention also launched overtures to the French and Dutch, possible allies in the coming struggle. For years, the mantra "No taxation without representation" prevailed. By '76, armed with the solidarity generated within the gathering in Pennsylvania, the colonies were ready to go it alone—toward a new and independent nation. From the reflexiveness of resistance to the confrontation in colony after colony, the reality of revolution finally emerged, symbolized by the widely repeated image of the Liberty Tree.

The Content and Spirit of the Declaration

For purposes of this book, the indisputably pre-eminent milestone of the age, both for Americans and subsequently the French, was the Declaration of Independence. Few documents in history have so briefly summed up the animating ideas leading to political action of so dramatic a kind. As a manifesto, the Declaration needs but eleven lines to accomplish its aim. As a complete bill of indictment against British authority, it takes two full pages in modern type to cover.

"A Declaration by the Representatives of the United States of America; in Congress Assembled, July 3, 1776."

> We hold these truths to be self-evident, that all men are created equal, that they are endowed by their creator with certain unalienable rights, that among these are life, liberty and the pursuit of happiness; that to secure these rights, governments are instituted among men, deriving their just powers from the consent of the governed; that whenever any form of government becomes destructive of these ends, it is the right of the people to alter or to abolish it and to institute new government, laying its foundation on such principles and organizing its powers in such form, as to the them shall seem most likely to effect their safety and happiness...

It is the unabashed assertion of equality of human beings that makes the manifesto so powerful, for on it rest the other thrusts, of rights to security, freedom, and personal autonomy. These, in turn, justify the place of government in our lives. Without our consent, however, government has no justification or legitimacy.

In these briefly stated claims, two of Rousseau's ideas stand out, namely, that equality is the necessary concept for recognizing the twin facets of human nature. On the one hand, we have separate and individual selves and are built to defend those. This in spite of the fact that historically the individual had real social identity only by status of birth and place.

We also have, Rousseau wrote, the need and capacity for cooperation with others. Where these two attributes come together, in that interface, is where we begin to consider what kind of agency can compose the encounter and accommodate both through institutions of shared design. The Declaration sees it no less clearly than did Rousseau: the consent of the governed (the general will) is the key to any organization that can endure without defaulting into tyranny.

Jefferson and his fellow drafters in Philadelphia grounded their claims in natural rights as expressions of a divine endowment in man's reason. Rousseau engaged the realm of nature very differently, less metaphysically. Nature, in short, can remind of us what we are, but it cannot ordain what we do or how we should proceed to live together in peace.

While there's apparently no evidence of Rousseau's explicit influence on Jefferson's understanding of equality, there is a record of collateral effect through contemporaries Claude Adrien Helvetius (*De l'esprit*, 1758) and Francis Hutcheson (*System of Moral Philosophy*, 1755). Both of these men believed that the moral faculty was uniformly or equally distributed and that compromised education or the conditions of an individual life could distort that capacity. Man's moral sense is his highest faculty, which, according to Garry Wills, Jefferson once described as "the brightest gem with which the human character is studded."[13] Wills goes on to add: "To say that men are equal in their exercise of this faculty is to define them as *essentially* equal, for the moral sense is what makes man accountable to himself and others, self-governing and consenting to social obligation."[14]

Inclusive or Exclusive Coverage?

But wait, wasn't Jefferson's vision of equality limited to White people? Well, yes, of course, in his personal and common practice, and all but completely in theory. Wills reminds us that Jefferson owned a plantation like several of his fellow Virginia leaders, and he points out that the constraints of his chronic debt and unwillingness to pay the price of manumission were stronger than his interest in science and observation of the natural world. Easy to dismiss as a hypocrite? Wills doesn't avoid the term, but he gives us another insight, too. A fuller understanding of Jefferson's views points to a universal *moral sense* or character among mankind. "It is enough for now to see that [Jefferson's] political beliefs grew directly from the philosophy of moral sense, which had egalitarianism as an essential ingredient; and that his statements on black disabilities [*sic; deficiencies?*] are not inconsistent with that egalitarian philosophy."[15] The following paragraph comes from Jefferson the empiricist philosopher:

> Whether further observation will or will not verify the conjecture that nature has been less bountiful to [Blacks] in the endowments of the head, I believe that in those of the heart she will be found to have done them justice. That disposition to theft with which they have been found branded, must be ascribed to their situation, and not to any depravity of the moral sense...We find among them numerous instances of the most rigid integrity, and as many as among their better instructed masters of benevolence, gratitude and unshaken fidelity.[16]

The dark presence of racial exclusivity in the Declaration as implicitly understood at the time of its drafting became patently obvious to history

---

[13] Garry Wills, *Inventing America, Jefferson's Declaration of Independence,* (New York: Vintage, 1979), 211.
[14] Wills, *Inventing America,* 211.
[15] Wills, 228.
[16] Wills, 223-4

when the time comes for drafting the Constitution eleven years later. But that flaw would not be formally redressed as national policy for another ninety years.

Other Explanations for the Equality Clause

Jefferson's journal, as Wills tells us, includes a note on the disparity in voting power of British home-landers vs. colonials in America, in which he demands to know why a fraction of eligible voters in Great Britain—he estimated fewer than 200,000—should "give law" to four million here.[17] Arguably, we might understand this as redressing the in-equality of rights and power of citizenship between colonial Americans and their British cousins. Americans had long assumed, and certainly acted as though, they had rights as subjects of English law. And in fact, colonial courts had a good deal of autonomy with local enforcement, subject ultimately in special appeal to the Privy Council in London. It was this tradition, suggests Flavell in *When London Was Capital of America*, that colonials believed was violated by recent acts of Parliament and decrees of the crown.

Humanistic studies scholar Danielle Allen supports this interpretation in her exhaustive work *Our Declaration: A Reading of the Declaration of Independence in Defense of Equality* (2010). She sees the claim of independence as merely one of five instances where the Declaration stakes claims for equality—for the foundation of freedom can only be derived from the people themselves. By pledging to one another "their lives, their fortunes and their sacred honor," the signers "anted up" and claimed an equal "ownership share" of a new political order, one in which reciprocal commitments are made to work out its promises together.[18] As Allen succinctly states in the first lines of her Epilogue, "The Declaration of Independence makes a coherent philosophical argument from start to finish. It is this: equality has precedence over freedom; only on the basis of equality can freedom be securely achieved."[19]

Before addressing reaction from other countries to the Declaration both in the late eighteenth century and since, a couple of facts about its domestic history warrant attention. Garry Wills tells us that public notice, let alone celebration of the Declaration, was scant at first.[20] Since then, the Declaration has become an icon of symbolism for patriotic outpourings of all kinds. For

---

[17] Wills, 207.

[18] Danielle Allen, *Our Declaration: A Reading of the Declaration of Independence in Defense of Equality*, (New York: Liveright Publishing Company, 2010), 268.

[19] Allen, *Our Declaration*, 275.

[20] Wills, 324.

example, Abraham Lincoln's rhetorical usage of its Preamble in his Gettys-burg address gave a significant boost to the Declaration's popular image.

One of the explanatory propositions circulating near the time of its drafting was of immense practicality and had to do with public finance. Wills goes on to note that under international law, the formal act of separa-tion from Britain gave the colonies formal status as states, making it possible for foreign countries to extend developmental loans or credit.[21]

Despite achieving internationally legal status to command attention of creditors, the proposition still lacked practicality. Each colony guarded its individual independence and did not automatically subscribe to or authorize a union of colonies. It would take over a year to convention again and, in 1777, adopt the Articles of Confederation. Moreover, the law of nations required that an existing nation-state recognize these new states, either individu-ally or as a collective. That step would have to await the completion of a treaty. John Adams headed the negotiations that would produce The Treaty of Paris, drafted in 1782 in Paris, and signed in early 1783. Later that year, in a set of treaties known as the Peace of Paris, the United States and Britain formally concluded their armed conflict and defined the territory ceded by Britain to the United States.

The French Experience in the Eighteenth Century

A common inheritance of both the American and French Revolutions included the ideas born of the Enlightenment's major writings, yet the contexts of their application were very different. In France, one's rights and freedoms depended on which *estate* (nobility, clerical or commoner) one occupied at birth or achieved through the intervention of a sponsoring patron or institution like the Church. Resistance to and removal of those imposed distinctions gave the Revolution its first form. In America, on other hand, those indelible marks of feudalism never had a place. Instead, the colo-nists sought "home rule"—the power to administer on their own what was already present in the overlay of English law.

This divergence in contexts illustrates that the French carried out a revo-lution not merely political in nature but also cultural. The changes implied the felt need to upend a way of life: deference to and domination by rela-tively few over many more. And the distinction makes the French example a genuine *revolution* whereas the American resort to arms, more characteristic

---

[21] Wills, 324-5.

of civil war or a revolt, had more the limited aims of seeking a change of government, or, in the parlance of very modern times, a "regime change."

The two revolutions shared one notable similarity, in that economic forces—specifically the cost of imperial defense—stimulated both movements. Just as Britain sought to tax its colonists for support in the war with France, so too did the king of France seek to tax his subjects more in order to shore up the finances of his kingdom. Some of the depletion of Louis XVI's treasury in 1788–89 could be attributed to the recently concluded war with Britain, as well as France's direct support of the Americans. The king and his advisors willingly bore the cost in the late 1770s, once the Americans prevailed over the British in major battles like the one at Saratoga, New York.

The finances of the kingdom of France were so exhausted that Louis XVI urgently tried to raise taxes through a virtual mobilization. He summoned the Estates General, a body composed of representatives or deputies from the country's three broad segments or estates: nobility, clergy and commons. The Estates General had not met for over a hundred years. The assembly soon foundered with regard to the king's plan, when discourse—led by the commons, or Third Estate—devolved into extensive airing of grievances like the price of grain in a year of poor harvests. The Third Estate, with enough proportional votes, then declared themselves the new National Assembly and offered the king a new arrangement.

When push came to shove, Louis XVI did not agree to a new constitution requiring him to share power with the National Assembly, and he subsequently ordered his troops to surround Versailles, where the assembly awaited his response. The next day, July 14, Parisians stormed the Bastille in protest. While the symbolic significance of liberating a prison for political prisoners of the crown seems obvious, the practical significance lies in the prospect of liberating arms and gun powder for the rebellion. France thus began its Revolution.[22] And in the moment, too, the French nation created one of its most enduring images.

The urban setting of the resort to arms should not disguise the rural thrust of the early claims made for the revolution. According to R.H. Tawney, four-fifths of the French population lived and worked on the land at that time. He notes in *Equality* that the originating principal aim of the French Revo-

---

[22] Just as enduring are the blue, white and red of the French Tricolor which replaced the royal standard of black *fleur de lis* on a plain field of white. No less important is the stirring national anthem *La Marseillaise*, sung for the first time in Strasbourg on April 25, 1792. J. Llewellyn and S. Thompson, "French Revolution timeline 1789", Alpha History, accessed 4 September 2020, https://alphahistory.com/frenchrevolution/french-revolution-timeline-1789/.

lution was fairly simple and conservative. No one set out to overthrow the monarchy or to re-distribute land, although both things would happen in the next two years. Rather, the revolution began as an attack on the privileges and economic advantages built into the stratified social order and imposed by French law. The initial uprising railed against juristic and not primarily economic inequality—against differences in the legal status of the mostly noble land owners, compared to those who worked on that land.

The National Assembly took dramatic steps to complete the assault on privilege in the later months of 1789, which included nationalizing the land holdings of the Roman Catholic Church. The move both paid off national debt and financed widespread land distribution. While peasant landowners—those without titles, and some farmers—could buy property through the government's issue of bonds (*assignats*), ironically the money fell short, partly because their speculation let to inflation.[23]

Legacies

For purposes of this book, the distinctive legacy of the French Revolution lies in the visionary character of the Declaration of the Rights of Man and Citizen, adopted by the National Assembly in August of 1789, little more than a month after the storming and destruction of the Bastille. It predated and foreshadowed the adoption of a series of constitutions through 1793 and informed a part of each. At a glance the language of its seventeen articles strongly resembles parts of the American Declaration of Independence, notably regarding the weight given liberty and equality. Except there's more. The French Declaration includes protection of freedom of expression and religion not explicitly safeguarded for Americans until the Bill of Rights was ratified in 1791.

Here are core fundamental enumerated principles from *The Declaration of the Rights of Man and Citizen* interspersed with the author's notes for comparison with their American equivalents or approximations:

---

[23] In 1790 the assembly finished the work of dis-establishing feudal nobility by legislatively abolishing all hereditary titles. The strong identity with social as well as economic equality vividly colored these first two years of the Revolution. (See *The French Revolution*, "The New Regime," in Britannica Online Encyclopedia pages 1-4, https://www.britannica.com/event/French-Revolution/The-new-regime. The Revolution had created its own guidebook. It remained for a myriad of those who had drafted it and a host of others to implement its principles. One way they tried to do this was by incorporating the Declaration in successive versions of the French Constitution, both the one creating a constitutional monarchy and later ones declaring a republic.

"I. Men are born, and always continue, free and equal in respect of their rights. Civil distinctions, therefore, can only be founded on public utility."[24]

The first sentence reflects the claims of the Preamble to the American Declaration of Independence. The second is novel or brand new; it probably was simply intended to permit unofficial distinctions of the professions such as lawyer or doctor. It could also anticipate the public need of commissions to army officers, diplomats and magistrates. The presence of this second sentence in Article 1 is striking to an American because neither colonial governments nor those under our Constitution permitted or permits the granting of titles of nobility. The French, however, did have such titles and so here we see the advanced recognition that some medals or other distinctions might be appropriate but only where they are "founded on public utility." It could also be construed as allowing Parliament to award medals of honor for distinguished service in the military or the sciences, for example.

"II. The end of all political associations is the preservation of the natural and imprescriptible rights of man; and these rights are Liberty, Property, Security, and Resistance of Oppression."[25]

While this partially reflects America's Declaration, it substitutes property rights for the "pursuit of happiness," striking a slightly more conservative tone than in America's founding documents save for the Fifth Amendment that specifies "no taking" without due process of law.

"III. The Nation is essentially the source of all sovereignty; nor can any individual, or any body of men, be entitled to any authority which is not expressly derived from it."[26]

The French apparently sought to make it clear there would be no claim recognized in France on behalf of another "authority" beyond that of the French nation-state, such as the Catholic Church.

"IV. Political Liberty consists in the power of doing whatever does not injure another. The exercise of the natural rights of every man has no other limits than those which are necessary to secure to every other man the free exercise of the same rights; and these limits are determinable only by the law."[27]

---

[24] George L. Abernathy, ed., *The Idea of Equality, An Anthology* (Richmond, VA: John Knox Press, 1959), 156.
[25] Abernathy, 156.
[26] Abernathy, 156.
[27] Abernathy, 156-7.

This explicit article underscores individualism while affirming equality before the law, while said individualism is merely implicit in the canons of Anglo-American jurisprudence.

...

"VI. The law is an expression of the will of the community. All citizens have a right to concur, either personally or by their representatives, in its formation. It should be the same to all, whether it protects or punishes; and all being equal in its sight, are equally eligible to all honors, places, and employments, according to their different abilities, without any other distinction than that created by their virtues and talents."[28]

The framers take the twin ideas of equality before the law and the democratic process by which the law is determined and they emphasize, more so than the American framers, the "consent of the governed" which not only permits but expects participation from members of the same community. As Simon Schama notes in *Citizens: A Chronicle of the French Revolution*, this interpretation reflects what Rousseau conceived as the appropriate social contract for replacing the "arbitrary divisions of custom and habit" with "rational, equalizing institutions [to put] men into relations with one another as citizens, bound by the same sovereignty: their own."[29]

...

"XI. The unrestrained communication of thoughts and opinions being one of the most precious Rights of Man, every citizen may speak, write, and publish freely, provided he is responsible for the abuse of this liberty, in cases determined by the law. "[30]

This article certainly reflects the freedom of speech and press guaranteed to Americans in the First Amendment. The French however, once again, more explicitly delineate limitations only spelled out gradually in the United States through case law, such as speech that defames someone or incites riot.[31]

Although many of the concepts in the Declaration of the Rights of Man seem familiar, it is not obvious to us now how the American experience of its revolutionary founding could have influenced the French when the American Bill of Rights had not yet been formally adopted. As it turns out, our state

---

[28] Abernathy, 157.

[29] Simon Schama, *Citizens: A Chronicle of the French Revolution*, (New York: Vintage, 1989), 475.

[30] Abernathy, 157.

[31] Johnson, Vincent Robert. "The French Declaration of the Rights of Man and Citizen of 1789." *Boston College International and Comparative Law Review* 13, no. 1 (December 1990), 35.

constitutions in those critical years following 1776 contained many of these ideas. Thoughtful Frenchmen—paying attention to many things American, especially those affecting France's timeless adversary, the English—read individual state constitutions. Benjamin Franklin had a hand in this, too, circulating copies of the Declaration of Independence as well as copies of earlier versions of bills of rights imbedded in comparable state documents.

One of Franklin's most notable cooperating figures was the Marquis de Lafayette, lately returned from his distinctive military service in George Washington's continental army. Lafayette contacted James Madison for comments on his draft and subsequently submitted it to the French National Assembly.[32]

The revolutionary summer of 1789 resulted in a number of specific legal changes reflected among the aspirations of the Declaration of the Rights of Man. In the same fateful month of August, 1789, the National Assembly voted to abolish the feudal privileges of the nobility, ended priestly immunity from taxation, and proclaimed freedom of speech and for religious opinion. Historian Johnathan Israel considers the French Revolution "a stunning success... For the first time in history, equality, individual liberty, the right to equal protection by the state, and freedom of thought and expression were enshrined as basic principles declared inherent in all just and rational societies The bedrock of democratic modernity was in place."[33]

However promising the ideals the French put forth in their declaration, to say, as Jonathan Israel does, that they were "enshrined as basic principles," does not mean anyone put them into effect. All too often the ideals were ignored, overwhelmed or suspended by one group or another. In 1792, the monarchy was abolished with the founding of the first Republic of France, and 1793 saw the king tried, convicted and executed for conspiring against public liberty. For several years thereafter, France lived through a nightmare of ideological and factional warfare—not to mention several real wars with other countries—and deadly revenge. Factionalism spread and the most radical of leaders came to power. Under Maximillian de Robespierre (1758-1794), the Terror grew to shadow the revolution in ways that remain troubling to all who have been inspired by its stated ideals.

The period derives its continued notoriety from the image of the state's singular instrument of terror, the guillotine. It seems fair to say that none of the "heroes of the Revolution" in the first annual celebration on July 14,

---

[32] Johnson, "The French Declaration" 11-13.

[33] Jonathan Israel, *Revolutionary Ideas, An Intellectual History of the French Revolution from the "Rights of Man" to Robespierre.* (Princeton: Princeton University Press, 2014), 84.

1790, could have anticipated or welcomed these developments. Likenesses in a bust and medallions were paraded in the streets of Paris on that day of Rousseau, Voltaire and Franklin.[34] Neither equality nor liberty was advanced but rather they were curtailed, as French citizens experienced widespread insecurity in a steady state of turmoil.

What then is to be made of the madness of the Terror and related debasement of civil rights in those years? Could a stronger tradition of an independent judiciary have made a difference? Certainly before this time France did not enjoy anything comparable to what American courts possessed even in their colonial period. Recent legal scholarship suggests that it's an unrealistic question, given France's thousand years of monarchy and parallel sources of authority in baronial and ecclesiastical courts.

Writing in 1990 about the French Declaration and its historic setting, law professor Vincent Robert Johnson contends that the "protection of civil rights is an act of governmental maturity and willingness to embrace the ideal of the rule of law, as is well evident to anyone who looks around the world today."[35]

The future of the revolutionary ideals of both the French in their break from the medieval past and the Americans in their project for a new nation remained, at the end of that century, challenges for the world to study and sometimes to follow. In the following chapters various features of those ideals will surface again and again but rarely in uncomplicated ways. Many new social and political terms were spawned by these revolutions—such as *ideologue, partisanship, left vs. right*. The one that we explore in the next chapter—*reaction*—like other contributions from both physics and political philosophy, captures something of the uncharted dynamic revealed in this two hundred year survey.

---

[34] Israel, 84.
[35] Johnson, "The French Declaration," 32.

Chapter Three: Reaction

Equality's Shadow[36]

Theory and practice can take very different forms over time while reflecting the influence of ideas within concrete developments. Americans took five years to complete their fight for independence, but within a few years thereafter they had built an institutional edifice out of the stuff of reason, experience, and verbal struggle. The French, on the other hand, started with a wider set of ideals but then had to endure ten years of civil conflict plus the distraction of foreign wars as well. Only after the closure of the Napoleonic imperial period did the French find their way to building on the ideals declared in 1789. The translation of such an extensive collection of ideas into political or legal reality would take more time.

What can revolutions teach us about promoting and practicing ideas that support lasting civic harmony? Because the course of the long-running French Revolution produced so much bloodiness, betrayal, and out-right suppression, it has had to endure one more infamy: most revolutions since then are all but guaranteed to end badly, producing more harm than good.

Consider Felix Gilbert's assessment:

> Revolution became a destructive force which threatened the security, the property, even the life of every individual. Ever since Burke and since the Terror, fear of revolution has been one of the persistent elements in the Western Political atmosphere...The development

---

[36] And liberty's shadow, too, as seen so clearly in 1790s England.

from monarchy to anarchy, to terror and then to military despotism was presented as unavoidable once the orderly road of law was abandoned...[T]he idea of a cycle through which a revolution will end in dictatorship of a military man was not only an anti-revolutionary argument of conservatives but was generally regarded as a possibility actually inherent in any revolutionary movement.[37]

Edmund Burke published *Reflections on the Revolution in France* in 1790, not waiting for the turmoil of two years later, apparently convinced that nothing good would come from the abstractions contained in the French Declaration of the previous year. Burke clearly targets his fellow countrymen and their beliefs. He especially aims to disparage Richard Price (1723–1791), a non-Anglican preacher, for a sermon eloquently supportive of the French Declaration. Burke criticizes both Price's propositions and his use of the pulpit to deliver them. Price—referring to the so-called Glorious Revolution of 1688, the settlement of a new line of inherited sovereigns from Holland—claims that the English king owes his crown to his people. According to "this spiritual doctor of politics," Burke maintains, "if his majesty does not owe his crown to the people, he is no *lawful king*. Now nothing can be more untrue than that the crown of this kingdom is so held by his Majesty."[38]

Burke might not have considered that efforts at liberalizing reforms in Parliament could happen traditionally, with the Crown and Parliament working together. Nor was he expressly exercised about the influence of the new American republic just a decade earlier.[39] He was clearly concerned, however, about the sanctity and permanence of the English monarchy. Price's sentiments, he argues, are more than mere "theory pickled in the preserving juices of pulpit eloquence and laid by for future use."[40] Repeated "habitually," such expressions would come to appear to congregants as "a first prin-

---

[37] Felix Gilbert "Revolution." In *Dictionary of the History of Ideas IV*, edited by Philip P. Wiener, (New York: Scribner's, 1973), 152,157.

[38] Edmund Burke. "Reflections on the Revolution in France," in Vol. 24 of *The Harvard Classics*, (New York: P.F. Collier and Son, 1909) 151.

[39] Keeping track of controversial figures like Price could have been merely episodic with Burke, yet he likely did know of his vocal support for American independence. Price, a frequent correspondent of Benjamin Franklin from the time they had met earlier in London, wrote in 1784 a letter of appreciation to him extolling the example that the American states had set for greater freedom in the world. See K.L. Penegar, *The Political Trial of Benjamin Franklin: Prelude to the American Revolution*, (New York: Algora Publishing, 2011), 110.

[40] Burke, "Reflections," 151.

ciple admitted without dispute."[41] And with that, whatever security popular opinion offers (our monarchy) will be "taken away."[42]

Lynn Hunt, in *Inventing Human Rights, A History*, claims that Burke's publication "gained instant recognition as the founding text of conservatism."[43] Burke took pains to trace Price's upsetting propositions to Jean-Jacques Rousseau. "We are not the converts of Rousseau... We know that we have made no discoveries, and we think that no discoveries are to be made in morality."[44]

However much Edmund Burke's assault on the revolution in France and the ideas at work in it represented or influenced many Britons of his time, others robustly challenged his views. Within the same year of Burke's publication, Mary Wollstonecraft (1759–1797) published *A Vindication of the Rights of Man*, simultaneously a direct rebuke of Burke and a defense of the French Revolution. Contrary to Burke, she expresses her appreciation for Rousseau's ideas, and she unabashedly challenges Burke about the place of morality if not in the old order of hierarchical authorities of crown, nobility and Church so clearly revered in *Reflections on the Revolution in France*.

Burke's views carried far more weight in 1790s England than those of his detractors. Nevertheless, as Mark Philp notes in the 2013 introduction to William Godwin's *An Enquiry Concerning Political Justice*, together these other writers "spawned a huge pamphlet controversy"[45] (ix) regarding France and reform in Britain. The controversy, in turn, polarized opinion, which made the government more cautious about adopting measures against sedition. Parliament even suspended *habeas corpus*. When Britain declared war against France in 1793, reformers were branded as subversive French sympathizers. This period of anxiety, according to Philp, "pushed to the limits government's ability to retain order [in Ireland there was a rebellion and a French landing in 1798]."[46]

On its own, Burke's rosy take on Britain's constitutional history might well have been left to academic debate. In the wake, however, of the destructive turn the French took in the later years of their revolution, British sentiment and official action unsurprisingly turned defensive. Burke retains a distinctive cachet and identity, more often than not called conservatism.

---

[41] Burke, 151.

[42] Burke, 162.

[43] Lynn Hunt, *Inventing Human Rights, A History*, (New York: Norton, 2007), 17.

[44] Hunt, *Inventing Human Rights*, 17.

[45] Mark Philp, "Introduction," in *An Enquiry Concerning Political Justice* by William Godwin, (Oxford: Oxford World Classics, 2013), ix.

[46] Philp, "Introduction," ix.

Christopher Hitchens, in "Reactionary Prophet," suggests that "reactionary" may just as readily describe Burke. What's the difference, and why does it matter?

Reaction, according to Mark Lilla, first entered the vocabulary of European political thought in the eighteenth century and reflected both the scientific work of Isaac Newton—most notably his second law of motion—and the philosophical work of Montesquieu. Portraying political life as a dynamic, endless series of action and reactions, the French philosopher recognized if not the inevitably of revolutions, the possibility of them, even if there is no way to predict them, their outcomes or their reactions. Lilla, in his book *The Shipwrecked Mind: On Political Reaction*, identifies a reactionary as one who harbors a fixed point of reference—an earlier moment in history—when political or social life changed for the worse. Burke invokes what Lilla calls "political nostalgia,"[47] while addressing the early days of the French Revolution when the French broadly and boldly stated their aims, categorically rejecting the old order. Burke despised the rejection and feared for the attendant influence in his own country.

Alexis de Tocqueville (1805–1859) lived a couple of generations later than Burke, and that may have some explanatory value since he would not have personally endured the excesses of his father's generation. Nonetheless, he had a decidedly less dyspeptic view of the French Revolution. While he regretted and condemned the Reign of Terror and the Napoleonic wars, he appreciated/admired the heart of the revolution.

"Equality," Tocqueville believed, was the keynote of the age in which he lived, the "central dogma of a new social and political order," the capstone of a revolutionary attempt to "establish a social science, a philosophy."[48] He believed that a revolution based on the claims of political and social equality was but a part of history's growing or being led out of feudalism and into democracy.[49]

---

[47] Mark Lilla, *The Shipwrecked Mind: On Political Reaction*, (New York: The New York Review of Books, 2016), x.

[48] Sanford Lakoff, *Equality in Political Philosophy*, (Cambridge: Harvard University Press, 1964),158.

[49] Alexis de Tocqueville wrote two influential books; the later one on his country's overthrow of the 'old order' is our source: *The Old Regime and the Revolution 1856)*. His early one is better known by most Americans: *Democracy in America* (1831). An extended visit to the new United States led him to encounter the plain facts of material similarity among citizens of several states. Tocqueville noticed, too, how that condition seemingly expressed itself in the customs or mores of the time, especially the absence of any show of deference to officials or employers unlike what he knew to be the practice in Europe.

Whether any particular revolution will—or can—succeed remains speculative. The Terror clearly failed in France, but it needn't have, in Tocqueville's view. Reason itself was overwhelmed. What we do with that experience is the open question. To hold on to what was left behind, like titles of nobility and an established Church, remembered as sanctified by long presence, serves to diminish the imaginative capacity needed to envision a future without those things.

Philosopher Friedrich von Schlegel, Lilla reminds us, suggests that "[t]he historian is a backward looking prophet."[50] Do historians tell the future by looking backward? Is there any "neutrality" to be found among them? If not to capture some meaning for today, what is the justification for writing it in the first place? American historian Gordon Wood addresses that question in *The Purpose of the Past, Reflections on the Uses of History*. It is not that historians should ignore current issues, for they well may be "the stimulus for our forays into the past. It is natural for us to want to discover the sources, origins, of our present circumstances. But the present should not be the criterion for what we find in the past."[51]

History, critically researched and written, has few if any lessons for the present, Wood maintains. The best that effort can teach leaders of today is cautiousness about extrapolating from the past for guidance on today's issues. "Unlike sociology, political science, psychology and the other social sciences, which try to breed confidence in managing the future, history tends to inculcate skepticism about our ability to manipulate and control ... our destinies."[52]

None of these social sciences, we would readily admit, is ever finished or complete. If anything, science has taught us that we don't know what we don't know. So we keep trying to understand more fully the natural world as well as the realm surveyed by the softer sciences. Gordon Wood gives us the same kind of appraisal for the writing and reading of history. Its work is never finished; we keep trying to gain a more complete understanding of our past.[53]

---

[50] Lilla, *The Shipwrecked Mind*, 25.

[51] Gordon Wood, *The Purpose of the Past, Reflections on the Uses of History*, (New York: Penguin, 2008), 11.

[52] Wood, *Purpose of the Past*, 14

[53] *The Varieties of History: from Voltaire to the Present*, edited by Fritz Stern, (New York: Vintage Book 1973), is a set of conceptually organized essays which add weight and durability to the insight of Gordon Wood. A work that stresses the empiricism of the sciences as well as the actual struggles of people over time, a composition for the appreciation of ideas, is *The Western Intellectual Tradition, From Leonardo to Hegel* by J. Bronowski and Bruce Mazlish, (New York: Harper Colophon edition, 1975).

Sometimes new revelations or characterizations trouble the current generation. Our intellectual life is made up, Wood reminds us, of "struggles over getting people to accept different meanings of experience,"[54] as evidenced in Alexis de Tocqueville's visit to America amid its first generation of self-conscious Americans.

The French aristocrat, sometime international reporter, found a distinctive measure of equality among Americans both materially and socially. This was a time "when Americans were constructing their sense of nationhood—a sense of America as the land of enterprise and opportunity, as the place where anybody who works hard can make it."[55] Wood calls that sense of nationhood a "myth of identity" full blown by the time of Andrew Jackson but from which point "all subsequent American history seems to be receding."[56]

Wood's attention to the notion of an enduring national aspiration, the American dream, invites some further assessment of how reaction or myth-making or historic nostalgia is formed and carried forward over time. Who, for example, establishes the operative notions? Academics and other writers? What part do ordinary citizens play in that process?

Although he does not address those questions directly, political scientist Cory Robin, in *The Reactionary Mind*, demonstrates the dynamics at work in promoting distinctive understandings, interpretations, or "spin" of the past. In one example, opponents of reform use the tactics of the reformers. In the time of the French Revolution, ecclesiastics "stopped writing abstruse disquisitions for each other" and began sponsoring "accessible and popular defenses of religion" so that all "those who could read would have weapons against the assaults of ... turbulent philosophy."[57]

A second characteristic of the reactionary mind is more subtle, in Robin's view. Edmund Burke, for example, in his reaction to the French overthrow of the old regime of landed aristocracy, did not defend everything about it and even applauded the verve with which its excesses were assaulted. Namely, Burke claims, the nobility had grown "sluggish, inert and timid"—unable to defend itself from "the invasion of ability" from those with money from commerce in the cities of the country.[58] In other words the old guard was not acting the part of a governing elite. That's not to say there should not be any

---

[54] Wood, 129.
[55] Wood, 363.
[56] Wood, 363.
[57] Cory Robin, *The Reactionary Mind*, (New York: Oxford University Press, 2018), 47.
[58] Robin, *The Reactionary Mind*, 46.

elite, but this set had forfeited its chance by complacency. The conservative mind, Burke is telling us, fully expects to continue its influence in other ways and with expanded energy. We just have to be more energetic and imaginative. R.H. Tawney, writing in the twentieth century about the passage of the old order into one of commerce and industry, impliedly underscored Burke's point by identifying a new ethic of individual merit, one based, it was claimed, on competition and ability, replacing the older one of authority by custom and inheritance.[59]

---

[59] R.H. Tawney. *Equality*, (New York: Putnam/Capricorn, 1961), 104-05.

Chapter Four: The Juggernaut of Commerce

In the nineteenth century, the socio-economic scene changes dramatically from land and its produce to movable capital, commerce and cities. No more awkward mark of an old order lasted late into the nineteen century like the continued practice of slavery in much of the Americas. The accompanying trade in human beings from Africa and across the Atlantic remained, for some European leaders, a persistent embarrassment, made all the more difficult because commerce in human misery proved so profitable. This aspect of feudalism persisted where land—used for the growing of commodities—remained the principal asset. The land, much of it remote from the European capitals, consumed more labor than was available. Human captivity and enslavement as policy and practice in these places meant, among other things, that the conditions of work remained largely out of sight of those at the center of European social and political life.

Since 1650, British ships had transported almost three million Africans. By the end of the eighteenth century, Britain dominated the trade with an average of more than 150 slave ships leaving Liverpool, Bristol, and London every year. The slave-based economy of the British West Indies flourished, and its share of the world coffee and sugar production sustained Britain as she prepared for war with France in the 1790s.

In the history texts of the Anglophone world, this embarrassment becomes ripe for reform only after the ruptures produced by the French Revolution and its aftermath, and the wars of empire—especially those of the British versus the French—began to mend themselves. The efforts, for example, of William Wilberforce, motivated by his sense of Christian witness and mission, in concert with leading political lights like Granville

Sharp and William Pitt the Younger, had some rough going in Parliament. Anything seemingly tied to the revolutionary ideas of the French was suspect. And of course, as one could expect, overseas British planters and their inves-tors significantly opposed abating the slave trade, let alone abolition itself. Eventually, by the end of the first decade of the nineteenth century, Britain embarked on an almost singlehanded mission to make the Atlantic unsafe for slave trading ships, a remarkable expression of support for human equality in both scope and duration.

Meanwhile, across the Channel, the energy and spirit of the revolution in France, from its earliest expression of and for equality, led to the emancipa-tion of people of color faster than in any other country. While slavery was rare in metropolitan France, the enslaved of the many New World French colonies, especially the Caribbean, felt the impact almost immediately.

In 1788 prominent leaders of the Enlightenment formed a new associa-tion in Paris, La Société des Amis de Noirs—Society of the Friends of Blacks. Condorcet chaired the first meeting of the Society in 1789, and he issued a public statement calling for the immediate end of the slave trade between Africa and the New World. The debate in the French Assembly was fierce and, for a time, inconclusive. The ideals of freedom and equality espoused by many of its leaders met arguments decrying the betrayal of the national interests in maintaining strong, competitive commerce. Indeed, some of those speaking out against emancipation claimed that the Declaration of the Rights of Man applied only to the nation of France, not mankind at large. Moreover, could so many persons quickly released from the ignorance of bondage easily find their place among civilized society? Could not, instead, a gradual diminution of the number in slavery, a moratorium on importation, force plantation owners to treat their existing slaves better and with greater respect?

While the debates continued in Paris, news of the American Revolu-tion and its accompanying Declaration stirred unrest among slaves in the French colonies. In turn, the matter was forced to resolution in the National Convention. Two emancipation decrees emerged. The first, the General Emancipation decree, announced in August 1793, applied to the area north of St. Dominique, or what we now know as Haiti. The second Decree of the National Convention, in early 1794, officially abolished slavery in France and all of her territories. Local planters—often in concert with a portion of free Blacks who seemingly preferred the monarchy, or who did not trust the anti-clerical element of the revolution—as well the British in nearby slave-owning colonies, naturally felt threatened by these changes.

Napoleon, when he became First Consul of the Republic, tried to put the genie back in the bottle by issuing a Decree in 1802 re-establishing slavery in the Caribbean possessions. Little but continued chaos followed, and by 1804 Haiti, the most important colony by far, not only declared independence but eventually gained the recognition of European powers and the United States. Other French island possessions retained more protracted terms of colonial administrations.

Princeton's Johnathan Israel, in *Revolutionary Ideas, An Intellectual History of the French Revolution*, explains the paucity of historical commentary: "[t]he Caribbean Revolution, much underestimated and ignored, even by French writers, in the nineteenth and early twentieth centuries because it challenged European sway and primarily assisted blacks, in fact rapidly developed into an event of profound global significance."[60] Consider, for example, that a highly effective privateer fleet manned by recently freed slaves captured the merchant ships of Britain, Spain, and the young United States as prizes for the benefit of the French Republic. And expeditions were mounted by locals led by émigrés from France against places occupied by the British and Dutch, notably Grenada, Saint Vincent, and Curacao. There were even incursions onto the South American mainland of Venezuela.

In Britain and its American colonies, the first opposition to slavery and the slave trade came from the Quakers and similar groups of people moved by the inhumanity of both. Sidelined during the American Revolution and then, in Britain, by the shockwaves from the French Revolution, these efforts were eventually rewarded through an act of Parliament in 1807. By 1815, the Royal Navy regularly patrolled the coast of West Africa seizing those ships engaging in the trade and freeing the captives in ports where their security could be confirmed. The "Chasing Freedom" exhibit in the dockyard museum in Portsmouth, England, maintains that "[b]etween 1807 and 1860, the Royal Navy, West Africa Squadron seized approximately 1,600 ships involved in the slave trade and freed 150,000 Africans who were aboard these vessels." And yet, despite international treaties committing nations to end their slave trade, and condoning the interception of ships violating the ban, enforcement remained so incomplete that, according to some estimates, at least 1.5 million Africans arrived in the Americas during this period of lax enforcement.

The slave trade and the industries it supported accounted for only part of the Industrial Revolution. The spread of political participation in several

---

[60] Johnathan Israel, *Revolutionary Ideas, An Intellectual History of the French Revolution*, (Princeton: Princeton University Press, 2014), 414.

countries of Western Europe demonstrates the rise of associations looking to influence policies as well as attitudes. The nineteenth century would become the age of both individualism and socialism, of John Stuart Mill and Karl Marx. "Reactionary" got added to the political vocabulary. Herbert Spencer and Social Darwinism entered the mix. And institutions emerged that were fashioned in the wake of these ideas—labor unions, political parties, and agencies for relief of what the Victorians called urban distress.

In France, within thirty years, Rousseau had died, the revolution had ended, and Napoleon had not only risen but fallen, all while the Industrial Revolution steamed along, especially in Britain. By the turn of the century, thousands of mills or factories had changed the landscape, and Charles Dickens' satiric exposés of poorhouses and urban poverty were hardly needed to make their impact visible.

Thousands and thousands of former tenants or part time workers of farms and estates streamed into the new villages and towns forming around the new manufacturing plants. Most numerous, the textile mills spun cotton fiber and mechanically loomed cloth for Britons to wear and to export. Much if not most of the raw cotton came from the United States—a very profitable trade on both sides of the Atlantic, one that would continue to be so up to and beyond the American Civil War.

By 1785, Britain had begun to recover from the war in America and had not yet become involved with France in another. Despite financial capital aplenty for the expansion of textiles and other industries, finding workers to fill the mills and good sources of energy to run the new machinery remained a challenge. Increasingly, the mills and factories relied on both women and children to complete the workforce.

Although this was not typical, New Lanark in Scotland, situated on the headwaters of the Clyde River, had the remarkable convenience of water power at its doorstep. But if the Glasgow owners wanted to make the most of the site, they would need to import their labor, which is exactly what David Dale and Richard Arkwright did. They had four mills in operation by 1790, with a workforce of about 1,200, half of whom came from the orphanages of Edinburgh and Glasgow. The remainder of workers included families of Highlanders cleared from their tenancies within the last generation in remote parts of Scotland. Landowners had decided to maximize the income from their estates by raising sheep instead of sharing the meager returns from tenant cultivation alone, for cotton was not the only staple enjoying a boom in production. Many of the former tenant families found the prospect of relocating within their own country the lesser of two evils, as emigration to America clearly seemed more traumatic and uncertain.

Admittedly, we now know more about this particular set of textile mills—at its peak the largest in Scotland—than most others of the time, because of the social significance of its owners and operators. The original owners, David Dale and Richard Arkwright, built dormitories for their workers and families plus a nursery for the young children. Shifts ran thirteen hours a day, six days per week, and they did not become shorter for another ten years. What made New Lanark exceptional? Most of the workers were transplants, and the town offered few if any pubs or similar urban temptations. The big cities of Edinburgh and Glasgow were both miles away. Moreover, New Lanark maintained strict rules of employment; episodes of drunkenness or fighting could lead to discharge.

As fortune would have it, David Dale's daughter met and soon married a young Welshman named Robert Owen in the last year of the eighteenth century. By then, Owen, twenty-seven, had acquired both capital and plenty of experience in textile mills, having been apprenticed to an uncle in trade. At nineteen he became the manager of a mill in Manchester. Not formally educated, Owen, a serious reader, made good use of his uncle's ample library. Once married, he joined his father-in-law in management, and later, ownership of the New Lanark mills and property.

Dale and Owen shared the conviction that their commercial success required the wellbeing of their employees, an attitude Owen would hold even more decisively once he bought out the interests of his partners and ran the plants himself. Way ahead of his time in Britain, Owen proved a significant innovator. He built a school and set aside time early in the work day for the children's schooling and exercise, including dancing. He expanded the village store, set up originally by Dale, instituted a cooperative model, and used the profits to pay the teachers. He established an employee sick fund, and an adult education program called the Institution for the Formation of Character. Finally, he phased out child labor altogether.

Among his varied set of investors he counted Jeremy Bentham, the philosopher, and a number of notable Quakers in England. The world at-large noticed the goings-on at New Lanark. Owen's innovations caught the attention not only of investors but also of political leaders in Britain, and social reformers in Europe. Owen distinguished himself from most of his contemporary fellow industrialists by putting his ideas into print and talking about them with anyone willing to listen.

In 1814, he published A New View of Society Or, Essays on the Principle of the Formation of the Human Character, and the Application of the Principle to Practice, a collection of four essays. One directly answered the question about the rapidly deteriorating conditions of the cities: put more people to work in newly created self-sustaining villages—cooperatively operated along the lines of what New Lanark had done—and with the aid of scientific agriculture. His was a "plan of amelioration and reform without revolution."[61]

We might well trace a second essay to Rousseau's *Emile*. With little faith in economic or political reforms to bring sustained stability and growth, Owen believed we should first build the capacity for cooperation with fellow humans through education.

In his 1821 *Report to the County of Lanark*, Owen attacked the very idea of a society based on competition, and he derided the notion that only money could measure the value of work. He acknowledged the revolutionary character of the steam engine and other such inventions coming into use, but he argued strenuously that the gains were illusory. He considered those who profited from these advances monopolists—not ordinary people who tended the machines and did the remaining work of an increasingly complex economy.

We would be wrong to suppose that Owen's ideas fell on deaf ears. In time, various calls for worker organizations cropped up in major cities across Britain, especially those with concentrations of industry like Birmingham, Manchester, and Leeds. Perhaps Owen could foresee that in the future, politics would lead to confrontation and strife; and he had no appetite for it. He may well have had in mind the Peterloo Massacre of 1819, during which the cavalry charged into a crowd of thousands protesting in Manchester for Parliamentary district reform. Owen found concentrating on cooperative communities, and the opportunities for education in them, the better and probably safer route. Indeed, Owen was suspicious of efforts simply to expand voting rights to build a worker-dominated electorate. At one point he conceded that most of his fellow British citizens were not ready to direct their own destiny, at least not until they achieved a greater level of education. He felt that the nation, as a whole, would do well to institute cooperative villages like he had established in New Lanark, on a larger scale. But he left those details for another day, and others took up the call for labor unions.

---

[61] "Robert Owen," *Introduction to Contemporary Civilization in the West, A Source Book*, Columbia College Staff, eds., Vol. II, (New York: Columbia University Press,1946), 400-413.

Meanwhile, the Duke of Wellington, the general who had finally defeated Napoleon Bonaparte, and who stood for order, tradition and symbolism, held a firm hold in government for the remainder of the generation.

Robert Owen's life and ideas clearly straddled the centuries: born in the eighteenth, tested in the nineteenth, and anticipated for the twentieth. Not formally educated but widely read, Rousseau and Owen thought about some of the same things, particularly the importance of education and its capacity to engender mutual cooperation. But unlike Rousseau and his cohorts of the French Enlightenment, Owen had sustained experience among working people; from an early age he acquired the focused capacity of leadership among and on behalf of working people. Part patriarch? Perhaps. No one voted on his progressive innovations at New Lanark; he just put them into effect, confident everyone would benefit. Part idealist? Yes, for sure, Owen imagined the implications of improved conditions. Activist? Yes, to the lengths that his vision carried him.

The context of ideas that Owen lived in or hearkened to as he matured includes those of William Godwin, who studied the works of the French Enlightenment, among them Rousseau and Helvetius. Owen engaged with Godwin, author of the 1793 *An Inquiry Concerning Political Justice*, as well as the Reverend Richard Price, a dissenting clergyman in London who had spoken out on issues such as America's claims for independence, and enlisting the spirit of that cause for reforms in Britain. It is easy to neglect the collateral effect of the colonial Britons on those who wanted change in the mother country just as much.

Through Godwin, Owen also met Mary Wollstonecraft, noted at the time for her favorable view of the French Revolution written in response to Edmund Burke's very critical disparagement of it. What appears clearer now when we mention these works in the context of the changes that Owen set in motion is this: British leaders of opinion and policy did not merely react to the unprecedented events in France for their newsworthiness. Burke's message in 1790, nominally in the form of a letter to a friend in France, was well designed to condemn and push back against the increasing calls for reform in Britain itself. Owen, though of lesser literary fame, became a substantial part of the ferment that arguably put the two men on opposite sides of history.

Robert Owen believed enough in his ideas to boldly develop and demonstrate their efficacy in an altogether different material setting. He sold his share of the New Lanark mills to his partners, and with the proceeds he moved to the United States, where he purchased a large tract of land in the

Midwest and set up a cooperative village along the lines of one he'd sketched in his 1821 *Report*. In the spring of 1824, Owen, along with several of his sons, established New Harmony, Indiana, along the banks of the Wabash River. The utopian experiment did not quite work out as hoped. After three years, Owen returned to Britain and, for the next thirty years, concentrated on making the cooperative idea real—writing more and connecting with many others sharing a variety of interests. He never returned to Scotland but stationed himself in London, where the connections were most numerous and the prospects for larger change seemed bright.

Owen did not limit his investment in America to the founding of an experimental cooperative village in Indiana. Though he returned to Britain, his four sons and a daughter stayed and made distinctive contributions to their new country. Moreover, while he stayed a relatively short time in America, other communities emulated his New Harmony example. And even if none of them endured in original form for very long, he still inspired attempts to build a community of equals based on shared work and deliberate cultivation of the mind.

Liberty's Uncertain Landscape: Europe in the 1800s

For all the intellectual and social ferment in Britain at the start of the nineteenth century, as well as the war with France and a second war with the Americans (1812), the impact of France's late Revolution was negligible compared with what happened in most other European countries. Until the final defeat of Napoleon's army in 1815, the greater part of the continent was either under siege or occupation.

Reaching an imperialist version of "liberty, equality and fraternity" would never be easy given the widespread segments of resistance. For some, it meant trading one foreign king or emperor for another, such as when the Poles were ruled by Austria. For some others, there was a chance at carving out a separate cultural space from a larger territory, such as—Austria again the prime example—for Bohemians.

With the collapse of Napoleon's extended France, surviving monarchies did not relax. Instead they conceived a compact for their mutual protection: the Concert of Europe, hammered out in the Congress of Vienna in 1815. It would be their collective aim to guarantee that they would survive any future outbreaks of revolt. In "The Age of Reaction and Reconstruction, 1815–1865," Norman Sykes points out that "[t]he restoration of European order involved as a necessary corollary the suppression of centers of liberal and revolutionary thought. The proud age of enlightenment having ended in scenes of oppression and excess, an age of reaction was its natural successor."[62]

The diplomatic map of Europe was effectively redrawn with the emergence of a sense of shared interest among the crowned heads of state. That much had been learned from France's convulsions. It wasn't only that the French had terminated their monarchy—at least for some of the time after the Revolution—but they had executed their king as well.

For the next fifteen years Europe was composed, mostly at peace, and ready to get on with the usual business of top-down governance. The twin irritants to this state of things—economic inequality and unrepresentative government—however, did not disappear. The material conditions of most people did not improve but worsened as the effects of industrialism grew, much as they had done in Britain. When hardship increased—as it did in 1846–47—with failed harvests, so did the sense that a larger number of people were vulnerable. Resentment toward the rigidity of monarchy, and a growing appreciation of what the French had earlier promised themselves, expanded the cry for representative government.

All this came to a head by 1848 in what historians call the Workers' Spring.

The workers in question were, at the outset, those in Paris who staged protests when met with the cancellation of a popular skills training program—the National Workshops. Authorities responded with force and the workers threw up barricades. The army prevailed but not before the king, Louis Philippe, abdicated and fled to England.[63]

Landowners large and small, as well as farmers, resented the new land tax assessed to subsidize the costly National Workshops. Moreover, the tax proved hard to enforce. The outpouring of protest in the streets of Paris saw bloody clashes between disgruntled workers and the municipal guard, and regular army troops.

The three days of chaotic disruption in Paris strengthened the hand of conservatives in the provisional government, giving The Party of Order the dominant majority. National elections, announced for December of that same year, featured four candidates for president. The winner, with the broadest appeal to the widest segments of voters, was the one who seemed to have had

---

[62] Norman Sykes, "The Age of Reaction and Reconstruction, 1815-1865" in *Social and Political Ideas of the Age*, edited by F.J.C. Hearnshaw, (New York: Barnes and Noble, 1949), 9.

[63] David S. Mason, *A Concise History of Modern Europe*, (Lanham, MD: Rowman and Littlefield, 2011), 52.

the least probable chance. Yet, the cachet of his surname signaled a symbolic shift for France. Louis Napoléon, nephew of the great general, became the President of the Second French Republic at the end of 1848.

Not only did Louis have wide support in the villages and farms of the country—the yeomanry often being the backbone of conservative movements—but he won the vote of the lesser bourgeoisie of Paris and other cities. These shopkeepers and artisans, badly hit by the late recession and heavily in debt, resisted further reforms likely to complicate their return to prosperity. The election, however, clearly left the disgruntled unemployed workers more isolated than before.

This is the heart of the story of the French Revolutions of 1848—enough of the electorate saw the possibility of stability resumed or a respite from increased taxes to find a descendant of a one-time national hero preferable to the politicians of recent experience.

It is not surprising that the reactionaries won, you say. Aspects of liberty and equality both were frustrated. What else is significant about this story? Why does the very year—1848—stand out so vividly in the history of modern Europe?

Two themes have left an imprint on the history of equality as idea and as social-political dynamic: the importance of literature and the rise of national identity. In the first, the French experience of 1848, especially in June, has taken up a prominent place in, among other places, Romantic literature. Flaubert's novel *L'education sentimental* uses the revolutions of 1848 as backdrop. Russian author Dostoyevsky bears the marks of that time, as well. In his novel *The Brothers Karamazov*, one of the characters goes to Paris and joins the workers on the barricades.

The literature of politics and political philosophy flourished, too. Notably, both Friedrich Engels and Karl Marx were keen observers of those events. In his essay "The Eighteenth Brumaire of Louis Napoleon" (1852), Marx characterizes the 1848 revolution as a class struggle. Very few, if any, previous events of the age afford such a vivid sense of the kind of conflict that would infuse the language of reform movements and revolts for the next one hundred years, in places like 1917 Russia, 1930s Spain, 1949 China, and others. "[B]y the spring of 1848, revolutionary passion had infected Belgians, Italians, Hungarians, Germans, Bohemians, Dutch and Danes…The basic liberal principle of government by consent was steadily gaining influence as the middle class grew in size and influence."[64]

---

[64] Mason, *A Concise History*, 56-7.

Nationalism is not all of one sort. Political scientist Sanford Lakoff claims in *Ten Political Ideas that have Shaped the Modern World* that it can be both "centrifugal," as implied in the term Balkanization, and "centripetal," as in the German-language regions of central Europe.[65] Nationalism can also be civic or ethnic. Is either as consistent with tenets of democracy as the other? Lakoff argues that the civic kind is compatible with democracy, in theory, when the status of citizenship is open to all by birth or naturalization, regardless of ethnicity or religion or race. It is a shared commitment to identifiable symbols and ideals as well as living in a common territory that fulfills the promise of this kind of nationalism.[66]

If the ordinary people of France could find a strong voice for change, why not the Poles, too? Or the Italians, whose language stretched over the whole of that long peninsula but whose government took the form of a dozen different duchies or kingdoms? Or the fragmented German-speaking parts of central Europe? Eventually, over the next decade or so, these populations, especially the Italians and Germans, would find their way to coalescence into nation-states, stronger and more conscious of their cultural commonalities.

The re-shaping and consolidation of the map of Europe in the nineteenth century is of course a story of more than class structure and native consciousness. The parallel course of events also had to do with the material and economic forces at work. The very fact that the events of the spring of 1848 Paris, for example, could be reviewed in Warsaw, Frankfurt or Neapolitan newspapers the next day added to the sense of destiny shared. The telegraph, steam-powered rail systems, and a flowering literacy as well as the factories, mills, and mines all contributed to the rise in the general material wealth of the continent.

---

[65] Sanford Lakoff, *Ten Political Ideas That Have Shaped the Modern World*, (Lanham: Rowman & Littlefield, 2011), 149.

[66] Lakoff, *Ten Political Ideas*, 142.

CHAPTER FIVE: ANXIETY FOR THE INDIVIDUAL

The progressive visionary Robert Owen demonstrated how small cooperative communities might offset the mass production of factories and the corresponding social blight of cities. The plight of working men, women and their families engaged and challenged imaginative talents of varied stripes, some literary like Charles Dickens, others philosophical like Marx and Engel. Still others—like John Stuart Mill and Herbert Spencer in mid-nineteenth century Britain—tried to assess the political implications of these changes.

J.S. Mill

John Stuart Mill (1806–1873), a true contemporary of Tocqueville, thought the Frenchman mistakenly considered equality subversive of democracy. For starters, Mill did not see the individual claim for equality as being motivated by envy but rather as a demand for simple justice long denied under feudalism—or its remnants—in a stratified society like nineteenth-century Britain. In this condition, Mill argued, the enemy of individual liberty, the threat to its growth, lay not with the landed aristocracy so much as with the newly strengthened middle classes.

Mill saw that those bound to the land under the older regime of feudalism could, in his time, leave the land and seek employment in the city factories. They had the freedom to apply their labor to a job of choice and skill. But Mill also recognized that this new freedom was more theoretical than real. In commercial boom times, competition for labor of all degrees of skill level flourished, but in times of decline, factory owners had the freedom to discharge any and all workers at will. Having won equality before the law,

day laborers—versus tenant farmers, say— claimed no particular advantage regarding the equality of their condition, *except* they could now, with
whatever savings they might accumulate, acquire property, which offered
the potential for a better life, and for the most industrious or fortunate, even
wealth.

Mill and Alexis de Tocqueville shared the understanding that historically,
feudalism would give way to democracy. They both also possessed a deep
fear of and antipathy toward the centralization of power, like the monar-
chial regimes that France and Britain had either overthrown or transformed.
And both recognized that the great majority of the people were not ready to
fully participate in sharing power but that education across the classes alone
could advance the prospects for democratic government.

Yet they differed just as significantly in other respects. For Mill, the
distinctions—brought about by newfound wealth—posed a greater threat
to liberty than the leveling of conditions among men and classes. He saw
in his own country not a deadening uniformity of taste and aspiration, a
leveling of all societal distinctions, but rather the opposite. Mill's fear is
similar to Tocqueville's objection to the materialistic thrust of post-revolu-
tionary society, but Mill saw something positive in the rise of commerce and
industry.

Mills posited that as the middle class grew in power and influence, it
would become dominant, replacing the landed aristocracy of the old order.
This fluid middle class would also dominate taste, dictating that those so
inclined ascend to its ranks and join the traditional hierarchy, with attitudes
to match. Mill's insight pulled him in opposing directions. He lamented
the clamor for middle class advantages by those not yet in it. But Mill also
thought he saw, in the newly won freedom of mobility and legal equality,
the prospect for the real liberty of everyman to pursue his own ends. That
is what he understood as individualism, a force beyond that of Tocqueville's
vision.

It is that quality in people of any rank that promotes their rationality
and good judgment about who should lead, for example. It is individualism
that will counter tendencies to uniformity of opinion and help the free individual to resist the blight of ignorance and indifference. This aspect of Mill's
thinking owes something to Rousseau, especially the latter's emphasis on
education.

In the wake of the Industrial Revolution, Mill and other liberals of the
nineteenth century worried about the widespread deterioration in living
conditions. They could not explain or address this within the limits of the

liberal ethos—that of "one man, one vote"—which had not yet arrived in European societies, or the United States, for that matter. Human capacity for cooperation had not caught up with the selfish instincts that dominated the social conditions of nineteenth-century Europe.

Perhaps no one had a greater impact on our empathetic sense of the conditions in Victorian England than Charles Dickens. In his early novel *Oliver Twist*, we see up close the desperation of orphans held in the state's custody, something Dickens experienced when his father went to debtors' prison. He used the book to protest not only the policies but the institutions designed by the Poor Law of 1834 to confront family dissolution and homelessness as social problems. Dickens went on to give the same scathing, graphic account of the failures of public schools in *Hard Times* and of the legal system in *Bleak House*.

For Mill, like Rousseau, the capacity for reasoning and the ability to learn from experience could mitigate some personal deficiencies or obstacles and even improve one's conditions of existence. Neither man thought human nature immutable, nor did either of them ground his argument in abstract rights—from nature or any other source. Mill reckoned that when everyone acts to develop individual capacities fully, and does no harm to another, then society at large is better for it. In the book that secured his "lasting place in intellectual history"—*On Liberty*, 1859—Mill acknowledged his debt to contemporary thinker Wilhelm von Humboldt for the claim that "the end of man ... is the highest and most harmonious development of his powers."[67] And it is by that conviction we should judge all cultures and political systems, including economic ones.[68]

Equality for Mill was not the lodestar that it was for Rousseau, for whom the presence of feudalism was a continuing reality. He scarcely wrote about it affirmatively or as a separate principle, Lakoff contends in *Equality in Political Philosophy*, but as a corollary of individual liberty.[69] On the other hand, both men believed that the institutions we create or maintain can erode the promise of democratic governance to safeguard the liberty of the individual. For both, too, the success of a democratic state depended on man's ability to educate himself, develop a tolerance for opposing views and, in J. B. Schneewind's opinion, "sacrifice some ... immediate interests for the good

---

[67] Richard Reeves, *John Stuart Mill, Victorian Firebrand*, (London: Atlantic Books, 2007), 278.

[68] Following a period of emotional crisis in young adulthood, Mill realized that his own upbringing had been constricted but, according to Reeves, his education gave him the resources for his own fulfillment. That ultimate self-awareness, Reeves implies, lends his ideas their focus and lasting influence. *Victorian Firebrand*, 21-24.

[69] Lakoff, *Equality*, 138.

of society."[70] Mill's chief concern about democracy was that, Schneewind continues, a majority could become too powerful and suppress individuality, and the liberties of minorities; he makes particular reference to British Jews and women. Robert S. Dower tells us that Mill put his position to use, and while serving in the House of Commons Mill supported amendments to the 1867 Reform Bill that included extending the right to vote to women and establishing representation for minorities.[71]

Perhaps with pre-Revolutionary France in mind, Schneewind suggests, Mill insisted that "[d]emocratic tyranny would be far worse ... than aristocratic or despotic tyranny, since it would be far more effective in utilizing the most efficient means of social control, the pressure of public opinion." [72] His foresight of the eventual course of democracy in the twentieth and twenty-first centuries lends its own credence to his concerns.

Herbert Spencer

Overlapping with Mill's focus on the individual, a near contemporary saw meaning in equality but in a more limiting, abstract way. Herbert Spencer (1820–1903) occupies a unique place in philosophy. He paid little homage to Rousseau or to Hume and other members of that generation. His ideas came mainly from emerging sciences and their direct observation of nature. Precocious like Mill, Spencer found his education greatly influenced by his father and an uncle. Biology and psychology ranked high among his varied interests. He read Darwin carefully and even coined the phrase "survival of the fittest," a non-scientific term that has ever since shadowed the theories of natural selection and evolution. The younger Spencer mistrusted authority, both civil and religious, as did his father.

Spencer saw historic shifts like those from feudalism to democracy—or from a "law of status" society to one based on contract, a theory famously developed by Sir Henry Maine—as the continual adaptation of humanity to its conditions.[73] The individual with the better adaptive capacities would rise in both material and social advantage.

---

[70]*The Encyclopedia of Philosophy*, Vol. 5 (Macmillan and Free Press, 1997), 320.

[71]John Dower, "John Stuart Mill and the Philosophical Radicals," *Social and Political Ideas of Reaction and Reconstruction* (Barnes and Noble, 1949), 124.

[72] Schneewind, *Encyclopedia of Philosophy*, Vol. 5, 321.

[73] Sir Henry James Summer Maine, Ancient Law, Its Connection with the Early History of Society and Its Relation to Modern Ideas. (London: John Murray, 1861) in *Dictionary of the History of Ideas*, edited by Philip Paul Wiener, (New York: Charles Scribner's Sons, 1974) 2:61.

In a nutshell, Spencer's notion of equality—equality of freedom—develops only for those individuals who adapt best to the conditions of material and social life through all its evolutionary stages. Eventually, he thought, in some ideal stage—beyond his own industrial period at least—mankind will have become so well adapted to the competitive struggle it will attain an equilibrium that maintains social and economic conditions through contract and similar cooperative arrangements, not by state regulation.

Philosophy then, inferentially, must keep before us the prospect of such a society in the future. In the meantime, politics must preserve the greatest latitude for every individual to realize the potential of their every talent, strength and intelligence, even if in the interim those very differences will reward some and compromise others. Until then it is only necessary for government to avoid standing in the way of this process, by not preventing the most clever and talented, the hardest working, strivers from showing us the way.

Equality, then, in Spencer's view scarcely rises to the level of an ideal on the same plane as liberty. It does not bring with it a feeling of empathy for others because of their neediness or bad luck. It will come, when it comes, by dint of the force of social evolution. Only when we can all stand toe to toe with each other, not blinking, asking neither for mercy nor surrender, will we have the capacity to reach beyond ourselves and spontaneously embrace whatever common enterprise will benefit particular others. The best kind of cooperative society Spencer can hope for benefits not *most* people, or even many, but merely those who take up the competition. Spencer uses the notion of a social contract not as mythical construct but only to further the evolution of a future state of individuals and society—to assure that nothing the state does upsets the evolutionary progress already underway.

Referring to Southerners—like Virginia's George Fitzhugh on the eve of the Battle of Gettysburg, who, in the 1860s, intellectually engaged in an "attempt to roll back the Reformation in its political phases," Louis Hartz in *The Liberal Tradition in America* claims that Americans, even if they did not read the "European conservatives" like Spencer, wrote "uncannily as if they did."[74] According to Hartz, a central deficit in America's embrace of the liberalism borne of the Enlightenment and the French Revolution results from a lack of feudalism for liberalism to destroy. The related lack of emotive power and moral force significantly reduces not just equality but the essential element of fraternity.[75]

---

[74] Louis Hartz, *The Liberal Tradition in America*, (New York: Harcourt, 1991), 150
[75] Hartz, "*Liberal Tradition,*" 147-151.

When society or the electorate attempts to "[reproduce] the philosophy of a feudal world it has never seen," a kind of Reactionary Enlightenment, as Hartz calls it, arises. This phenomenon purports to see in the modern, liberally founded state the very embodiment of what all earlier struggles for liberty meant to overturn to insure that the individual remains sovereign, regardless of the character or existence of an implicit social contract, bringing us back to square one.

Herbert Spencer would see many political developments of the twentieth century, in both the U.S. and Europe, as seriously problematic, if not misguided. He would condemn publicly-subsidized health insurance, for example, or the forty-hour work week, as interference with natural selection. By simply putting off the emergence of equality of freedom, we obstruct the earlier arrival of an age of cooperation. He would consider these ad hoc adjustments—meant to make us feel better about workers who have little to show for their labor—as unscientific sentiment. That said, Spencer did, as Lakoff notes in his *Principles of Sociology*, acknowledge the plight of those in the sweatshops of his time, admitting that "[t]he wage-earning factory hand does indeed exemplify free labour [*sic*]...but this liberty amounts in practice to little more than the ability to exchange one slavery for another...since he has rarely an opportunity of doing anything more than decide in what mill he will pass the greater part of his dreary days."[76]

Mill, observing the same conditions, clearly expressed empathy and found a voice, ultimately, free from the aggregating calculus of Bentham's utilitarianism with which so much of his early years had been enthralled. Every individual must count, Mill insisted, for it is in the diversity of such talents and visions that each life in it enriches the whole of society.

Spencer, a purist in his individualism, did not compromise. Doctrinal analysis aside, Mill believed in a family of man composed of individuals whose latent talents and capacities can be encouraged, strengthened and expanded but only under conditions of freedom and a variety of stimuli. We don't have to wait for anything. What we need is already within us, enough in everyone for all of us to make those efforts. Together. Perhaps we can call Mill an optimist, or at least a pragmatist. For Spencer, equality only has meaning as it guarantees unqualified freedom for the individual—freedom to flourish if fit enough. If not, then the knowledge that an effort was made will have to suffice. While Spencer's lasting contribution in the canons of

---

[76] Lakoff, *Equality*, 144.

Western philosophy remains controversial, Lakoff contends, in *Ten Political Ideas That Have Shaped the Modern World*, that his theory at least fosters an insight about our intellectual inheritance from the Enlightenment. It is one thing to collect the knowledge that empirical science gives us; it is another to use it in fashioning policy proposals for governmental changes.[77]

In the same generation of J.S. Mill, an American author and lecturer of note was developing his own considerable reflections on the central theme shared between them then. "[D]estitute of faith but terrified of skepticism" says Michael Moran of the singular American exponent of individualism, Ralph Waldo Emerson (1803–1882).[78] Moran adds that Emerson was driven to discover for himself "an original relation to the universe" and not one derived either from the rationalism of the Enlightenment or the orthodoxy of the religious traditions of his native New England. Forsaking his original choice of careers as a minister in the Unitarian Church, he travelled widely in Europe and England. He met and formed a lasting friendship with Thomas Carlyle (1795–1881), whose influence he acknowledged.

Whereas Mill came to his identification with individualism through ethics and the prominence of political issues in his life, Emerson made the connection through his spiritualism and an active personal engagement with friends and associates. Both had a mistrust of democracy for at least one common reason: the induction of conformity to prevailing custom. Emerson, additionally, found the growing commercialism in American life stifling for the originality of the individual. Mill found similar conditions in England as a threat to liberty of thought and expression. As demonstrated in *Man and Man: The Social Philosophers*, both men have had ongoing influence—Mill for his political writings, principally *On Liberty*, and Emerson for his broadly appealing essays, ranging from "Self-Reliance" on personal integrity to "The Over-Soul" with its spark to the intellect, the will and the affections.[79]

While the three nineteenth century thinkers—Emerson, Mill and Spencer—have something in common, they have important differences as well. All of them see the individual human being as the instrument of civilization's enhancements of life and recipient as well of its benefits. There's no need to construct out of old myth or tradition a social contract with which

---

[77] Lakoff, *Ten Political Ideas*, 159-60.

[78] Michael Moran, "Emerson," *The Encyclopedia of Philosophy*, Vol. 2, (New York: Macmillan Publishing, 1967), 477, 478.

[79] Saxe Commins and Robert N. Linscott, eds., *Man and Man: The Social Philosophers*, (New York: Random House, 1947), 382-442.

to measure how well or poorly those enhancements are safeguarded or augmented. The spontaneous expressions of poets or essayists can provide inspiration for each of us to follow, whether or not they seek to influence particular events or life choices beyond our own. That is Emerson's chosen role, to be one of those inspired individuals. The grounding for that role could be spiritual—as to some extent it was in his case—or merely reflective of a force within. That role can be influenced of course by the persons and events of our separate lives, but it is the combination of resources mediated by our own aspirations that identify each individual's uniqueness. Emerson sought a role as critic or reformer, and his essays and lectures have been found to contain important insights of the issues of his time. Moreover, when moments of national concern pressed on his generation—most notably abolition of slavery—Emerson used his voice.[80]

Mill and Spencer played, albeit with differing scripts, a role as translators. They interpreted the legacy of a re-made social order dating back to at least the French Revolution. With feudalism overthrown and monarchy transformed, where not abolished, with greater equality of citizenship ushered into this new age, with liberty of conscience almost assured, the *what* and the *how* of social existence lay before them. What kind of new world map and compass would emerge from the old? And how would the independence of the individual be safeguarded from, say, the authority of the Church or State? For Mill, answering such questions necessarily drew him into political theory and practice. Liberalism was not his invention, of course, but it came into full bloom through his writings on liberty and limited government.

Herbert Spencer had studied biology, and he anticipated Darwin's theory of natural selection put forth in *The Origin of Species*. Confronted by the challenge of population growth popularized by Thomas Malthus (1766–1834), Spencer chose to take his awareness of post-revolution challenges into a kind of future-scape for the human species. For him there was, as yet, no solid foundation for building a society or polity better than what already existed. Nature has its own instruction to give, Spencer thought, and it would come into its own when human society as a whole had matured its constituent members into a better educated, more competent citizenry. Before that time, mankind should resist tinkering with political organization and simply strive to ensure that the state does not interfere with that inevitable process.

---

[80] See David M. Robinson, ed., *The Political Emerson*, (New York: Beacon Press, 2004).

While both Mill and Spencer believed that limited government meant restricting the state's encroachments on private property—the doctrine of laissez-faire—they differed in degree. Mill's willingness to engage with expedients of parliamentary reform and public assistance marked him as pragmatic. He was especially sensitive to the marginalization of women. In this division, Sanford Lakoff finds liberalism clearly "bifurcated into two wings, one commonly called liberal and [the other] conservative, divided mainly by disagreement over the economic role of government."[81] With that expansion of vision or growing sensitivity to compelling conditions—notably the plight of life in the industrialized cities—Mill acquired a lasting relevance beyond his time. Moreover, he found a voice for issues that transcended his own country. His outspokenness on America's institution of slavery was significant for he was both a philosopher and a sometime member of the British parliament, even as his support for the Union cause in the Civil War put him at odds with official British policy of neutrality.

[81] Lakoff, *Ten Political Ideas*, 71.

Chapter Six: Slavery's Abolition

The American Civil War presents a corollary to the increasing urbanization and manufacturing character of the American North contrasted with the traditional agricultural realms of the South. Slavery, in this context, represents the very antithesis of America as an emerging place of skilled or semi-skilled wage earners rather than the impetus for the four-year-long clash of arms and loss of a half million lives in a conflict often characterized as America's second revolution. At the core of the confrontation, between the older remnant of a quasi-feudal society in one region and the individualism and commercial initiative in the more dynamic North, lay the unfinished business of the Constitution and the later Bill of Rights—namely, the first ten amendments—and the utter abandonment of a considerable portion of the human inhabitants of the country.

Slavery in the New World was more than one hundred years old by the time of the American Revolution. Oldest in the colonies of the Portuguese and Spanish in South America, it developed later in those British colonies organized under the plantation system, like Maryland and the Carolinas. The very first slave ship to arrive in what is now the United States was Dutch. Its crew traded twenty African captives from the Caribbean for tobacco in Jamestown, Virginia. That was 1619, a year before the Puritans landed at Plymouth Rock with their pietistic hope for religious freedom from the established church in England. By the end of the seventeenth century, British slave ships dominated the sea, and by the time of the first official census of the new United States, 1790, the enslaved population had reached hundreds of thousands.

The 1700s saw economic growth of all kinds in the colonies, where the average citizen of New England lived better than a counterpart in the old country. Not so, however, for a sizable minority of residents of the southern colonies, who cultivated the profitable exports of tobacco, rice and indigo, and later cotton, as the British textile mills built a market for the fabric that was cheaper than linen or wool.

Slavery did not remain confined to the South. Benjamin Franklin and his wife Deborah, for example, in Philadelphia, owned several house servants.[82] While the British had never given the issue sustained attention as a Parliamentary concern, several pockets of public protest did exist: the Quakers of Pennsylvania; the church men of New England, like George Whitefield and Jonathan Edwards, caught up in the First Great Awakening (1730–1760s); and writers like Thomas Paine who, in 1775, published the widely circulated essay, "African Slavery in America."

The Society of Christian Friends, the Quakers, formed during the English Civil Wars of the mid-1600s, and they comprised part of the protest against orthodoxy and hierarchy in Britain. They fundamentally believe in the equality of souls—of both men and women—and that each human being embodies the spirit of God. That belief and consequent practice of sitting in silence without the leadership or direction of clergy led to intolerance and ostracism by other seventeenth-century Englishmen. In a great stroke of luck, the Friends obtained a royal grant of land in Pennsylvania, where they established a beachhead for tolerance and non-violence. Quakers enriched, if they didn't spawn, the Abolishment Movement with the very founding of their new Republic.

In a move that gave substantive legal form to the key claim of the Declaration of Independence—that all men are created equal—most of the newly formed states/former British colonies that lay north of the Ohio River and the Mason-Dixon Line abolished slavery. Once they claimed their own sovereignty, they acted decisively. Vermont in 1777 and Pennsylvania in 1780 became the very first to do so, preceding by a decade the French Revolution and adoption of the Declaration of the Rights of Man.

In Britain, too, abolitionists organized, calling first for the outlawing of the slave trade, as the popular press began reporting its brutality, and singling out major port cities like Bristol and Liverpool, home to hundreds of

---

[82] Walter Isaacson, Benjamin Franklin, *An American Life*, (New York: Simon & Schuster, 2003) 269.

slave ships. Just as in America, Quakers, and men like William Wilberforce, Thomas Clarkson and Granville Sharp, led the movement.[83]

Meanwhile, back in America, we must remind ourselves that Thomas Jefferson, during the drafting and ratification of the Constitution, was in France, serving as the first formal emissary of the United States to a major power. Had he been present in the Convention, would he have spoken out on the issues of slavery and the slave trade? Would he have felt pressed to explain how the claim in "his" Declaration of Independence that "all men are created equal" squared with the clear acceptance of slavery—but without the honesty to use the word—in the Constitution? Fully three different provisions of the document affect some aspect of slavery.

Of course we don't know the answer, but some of his fellow Virginians did share their views at the time. George Mason, though a slave owner himself, took to the floor in the ratification debate conducted in Virginia's Convention in 1788, and he condemned the provision in Article I, section 9, allowing the slave trade to continue for twenty years as "disgraceful to mankind."[84] When told that two of the states, South Carolina and Georgia, would not support the draft Constitution without such a provision, Mason said, "leave them out!" James Madison, chief architect of the draft and a tireless supporter of its adoption, appealed to Mason: "Great as the evil [of the slave trade] is, a dismemberment of the Union would be worse." Moreover, under the existing Articles of Confederation, the Congress would have no power to regulate the trade, so, Madison added, the provision actually offered "a step forward."[85]

Behind the scenes a current of opinion circulating in various northern states felt slavery would fade away with the passage of time. They could, in the meantime, deal with the issue of further supply; they could, in a gradual way, the reasoning went, squeeze the life from the institution. Additionally, mounting international pressure to address the slave trade issue seemed something the community of nations could agree on, feel good about as, Madison said, a step in the right direction.[86] The more basic issue of the

---

[83] In the early 1800s these British efforts were successful in building an international coalition against the slave trade, discussed in Chapter Four of this book. Those efforts did not, however, succeed in impelling Parliamentary action to abolish slavery in British West Indies colonies until 1833. Michael Taylor, "How the British Establishment Resisted the Abolition of Slavery," *The Times* (London), (Nov. 2020).

[84] Pauline Maier, *Ratification: The People Debate the Constitution 1787-1788*, (New York: Simon & Schuster, 2010), 283.

[85] Maier, *Ratification*, 284.

[86] The blockade to suppress the slave trade of 1807 is described in Chapter Four.

internal status of slaves, though, could and would not be taken up in the drafting and ratification exercise of 1787–88.

The drafters and supporters showed their willingness to launch their country with a deep moral fault line running right between its two halves. Having swallowed that contradiction, the founders trapped themselves into accepting others. Article IV, Section 3, insured that persons "held to labor" in one state under that state's laws could not be "discharged" by "escaping into another." Rather, "they shall be delivered up on claim of the party to whom ... such labor is due."

What could be plainer? By this Constitution, the drafters promised to uphold slavery in the states that had it. Without this provision in Article IV, slave states could have contemplated a quicker end to their regime than anyone at the time might have imagined. Voting with their feet would have, quite conceivably, emptied those states of its productive work force in short order. How could a slave-tolerant society compete with freedom next door, down the road, or over the river?

By 1793, the Congress had doubled down on the Constitutional restriction and passed its first Fugitive Slave Act, which enabled owners to capture and remove "runaways" in otherwise free states and return them to their bondage in the South.

Any model of federalism promises more than a few problems of adjustment, but few could match the heated political controversies stemming from this central contradiction. Who would determine how to govern future growth? Would new territories become slave states or free? In late 1819, the state of Missouri applied for admission to the federal union as a slave state. At that point, we had an equal division: twenty-two states in each camp. To retain that balance, Congress enacted, in 1820, legislation that became known as the Missouri Compromise, granting admission simultaneously to Maine as a free state and to Missouri as slave.

Of the several places in the Constitution involving some dimension of slavery, probably the most cynical regards the aggregate number of persons counted for purposes of proportioned representatives in the House of Representatives. Per Article I, Section 3, those numbers "shall be determined by adding to the whole Number of free Persons, including those bound to Service for a Term of Years, and excluding Indians not taxed, three fifths of all other Persons."

For the single purpose of giving slave states enough political clout to reflect their economic strength and thus their collective bargaining power in Congress, the individual Black residents received a backhanded kind of recognition as partial people. Otherwise they counted not at all, not even on a par with European indentured servants—those merely "bound to service"— whose predominately voluntary contracts prescribed their freedoms. The racism of the charade shouts out at us in today's reading of the text.

One of the voices registering such outrage, albeit almost a century later, was that of a former slave who by that time had acquired sufficient public recognition for his words to remain with us.

> The Fourth of July is yours, not mine. You may rejoice, I must mourn. To drag a man in fetters into the grand illuminated temple of liberty, and call upon him to join you in joyous anthems, were inhuman mockery and sacrilegious irony. Do you mean, citizens, to mock me, by asking me to speak today?[87]

William Lloyd Garrison, mentor and early ally of Frederick Douglass, the best known leader of the abolitionist movement, began publishing *The Liberator* newspaper in 1831. Over time, however, they differed in tactics and ideas, because Garrison was convinced that the Union could not be preserved under the existing Constitution, although he believed in the opening lines of the Declaration of Independence for the nation's guidance. Douglass started his own newspaper and became the more popular orator, with a more forceful style of delivery rooted in his personal experience of slavery. By the time of Emancipation and the end of the War, they were re-united in the effort to secure voting rights through the Fifteenth Amendment.[88]

Douglass carried the same simple, direct message everywhere he went: as a nation we are not living up to the ideals of liberty and equality embodied in our founding documents; we must abolish slavery and give every man the vote. He called not for an uprising but for a change of heart among White people. His stance would put him at odds with John Brown of Kansas. And his advocacy for giving every man the vote would separate him from his suffrage friends Elizabeth Stanton and Susan B. Anthony. Douglass feared that combining abolition and votes for men *and women* in the same Constitutional amendment would mean failure for both causes. The Fifteenth Amendment would mark the achievement of his goal.

When war began, Douglass urged Lincoln to allow freedmen to serve in the Union Army. Surely nothing could have demonstrated more directly the patriotism of these new troops. Their presence in uniforms of blue must have

---

[87] July 5, 1852, Syracuse, NY, in David W. Blight, *Frederick Douglass: Prophet of Freedom*, (New York: Simon & Schuster, 2018),236.
[88] Blight, *Frederick Douglass*, 96, 202-216.

given heart to civilians and other federal troops all over the country, as well as mitigate the skepticism in the North regarding whether freedmen could be expected and/or trusted to carry out the requirements of citizenship.

Douglass had not expected Lincoln, on his own, to issue a Proclamation without a Congressional vote, so we can imagine his surprise when Lincoln did just that. At the same time, surely regret tempered his excitement, once he realized that the Proclamation applied only to those states still in "rebellion" and not to those occupied by Union forces or already re-admitted to the Union—like Kentucky, Maryland and Missouri and Tennessee—where slavery remained legal. As Commander-in-Chief and director of the War for Union, Lincoln had powers to strategically end the war, but not the powers of Congress to enact legislation.

Inspired by the open shore and broad sweep of the Chesapeake Bay bordering the eastern Maryland plantation of his childhood, Frederick Douglass dreamed of freedom. Seizing that freedom did not make him unique—for hundreds of others did it as well. Douglass, though, went on to become a world-renowned lecturer. And while runaways received various degrees of help along their way, Douglass received his first help from the lady of the Baltimore house in which he served. Mrs. Hugh Auld, Sophia, taught him to read and to write, patiently giving him time and attention with the books in the house. The tutelage came to an abrupt end when Mr. Auld discovered it, but Douglass carried on his education, reading newspapers he found in the city's streets.

Eventually, with the help of Anna Murray—a black Baltimore abolitionist and member of the Underground Railroad, who would become his first wife—Douglassmade his way out of Maryland and on to New York City in 1838, disguised as a sailor. He landed work in a publishing house and his writing flourished. Eventually Douglass would write and publish three books, *Narrative of the Life of Frederick Douglass, An American Slave* (1845); *My Bondage and My Freedom* (1855); and later, *Life and Times of Frederick Douglass* (1881). His ability to powerfully articulate not only his life story but the case for abolition made him one of the most celebrated orators, not just in his time, but in our nation's history.

In 1831 Massachusetts, William Lloyd Garrison, a principal ally of Douglass and leader of the abolitionist movement, began publishing *The Liberator* newspaper. In 1854, Garrison wrote:

> I am a believer in that portion of the Declaration of American Independence in which it is set forth, as among self-evident truths, "that

all men are created equal; that they are endowed by their Creator with certain inalienable rights; that among these are life, liberty, and the pursuit of happiness." Hence, I am an abolitionist. Hence, I cannot but regard oppression in every form—and most of all, that which turns a man into a thing—with indignation and abhorrence.[89]

Early on, Garrison encouraged women to become involved in the movement's leadership, providing opportunities for public speaking and organization as well as the writing and circulation of challenging pamphlets and articles. Two of Garrison's most active allies, Sarah and Angelina Grimke, privileged daughters of a patriarchal father, came from Charleston, South Carolina. At the age of five or six, Sarah later recalled, she witnessed the beating of a slave and the image never left her. Repulsed, she tried, unsuccessfully, to run away from home and board a steamboat from the wharves of Charleston. Denied formal education, Sarah read her father's law books instead. As a young woman, she accompanied her father to Philadelphia for his medical treatment, and she decided to stay. Her younger sister Angelina followed the same path, and together they joined the Quakers.

In 1836, the sisters moved to New York. They joined the Anti-Slavery Society, where they met William Lloyd Garrison after hearing him speak. Angelina's pamphlet, "Appeal to the Christian Women of the South," calls on her fellow Southerners to disobey their states' oppressive laws, teach their slaves to read, and set them free. Both sisters helped organize the 1837 Anti-Slavery Convention of Women which met in New York and hosted more than one hundred women from a dozen states. The next year, Angelina addressed a committee of the Massachusetts legislature, and she promoted a national stand against slavery.

A Network of Volunteers

The contradiction built solidly into the social and political fabric of the United States has no clearer demonstration than that extraordinary creation of social spontaneity known as the Underground Railroad. It ran its so-called lines across the divide between the region of slavery and the one of freedom. In operation from approximately 1830 through 1860, the volunteer network stretched across the boundaries of many states along the Mason Dixon Line and the Ohio River. Some stops, like Baltimore and Philadelphia in the East, and Cincinnati and Oberlin, Ohio, in the Midwest, became better known than others. No satisfactory count of the number of persons involved—either

---

[89] Blight, *Frederick Douglass*, 202-216.

as facilitators or passengers—exists, but the numbers climbed well into the hundreds of thousands.

The freedom waiting on the other side of the boundary depended critically on the human virtue of personal courage and the practiced arts of concealment and discretion. We might imagine the members, the keepers of safe houses and connections, as secure members of the majority community, but just as frequently they were freedmen and women living in precarious conditions. Similarly, not everyone who was intellectually committed to abolition possessed the requisite empathy to become "conductors" and "station masters." Some might assist a particular fugitive, if asked, but otherwise might not volunteer to help in such a direct, individual way; and those willing to flee might, likewise, question whom to trust along the way.

Advocates disagreed on ways and means, wondering, for example, if more energy and resources should go to political efforts—a legitimate concern. In 1816, the formation of a national American Colonization Society gave many abolitionists a scare. The Society wanted to use federal funds to resettle free Blacks in what is now Liberia, Africa. Only eighty-eight free persons of color elected to join the venture which, among other basics, lacked a defined territory and never received official support from its American sponsors. Remarkably, the territory survived, and by 1847 the settlers declared themselves a nation and sought recognition from European powers with other interests in the region. Great Britain, in 1848, became the first to recognize Liberia diplomatically. The United States government, conflicted in its own domestic politics, did not formally recognize Liberia until 1862, during the presidency of Abraham Lincoln. Following Haiti's example, Liberia launched only the second Black-administered republic in the world.

The next political strike against the abolitionists came with the passage in 1850 of a second Congressional Fugitive Slave Act. Under this latest legislation the owners of runaways could hire slave catchers and set them loose in the North to find and forcibly reclaim their "property." Sometimes these bounty hunters were careless or indifferent about authenticating identity, and they captured the "wrong ones." They kidnapped free persons of color, took them into the South for sale, or "returned" them to plantation owners.

Uncle Tom's Cabin

Not long after, in 1852, Harriet Beecher Stowe published her overnight best seller, *Uncle Tom's Cabin*. Her ally and friend Frederick Douglass wrote almost a year later that her book had reached "the universal soul of humanity."[90] It became the most popular novel in nineteenth-century America, and it sold well in Britain as well. Stowe, though a native of Connecticut, lived for a time in Cincinnati just across the Ohio River from Kentucky, a slave-holding state. Her husband taught at a local seminary. Both connected with those of the city involved in the Underground Railroad.

By her own account, several things influenced her to write the book, which was initially serialized in the abolitionist newspaper *National Era*. In addition to the most immediate impetus, the second Fugitive Slave Act, she also cited the accounts of freedmen, not to mention fugitives, who fled to Canada to avoid the reach of that law or its earlier version. Moreover, she might have found inspiration from the lives of the Grimke sisters, whom she would have encountered through Angelina Grimke's pamphlet, "Appeal to the Christian Women of the South." Their personal exposure to the brutality of slavery and willingness to respond would have been impressive to anyone even thinking soberly about what all the nation knew in one way or another. More explicitly than Grimke, however, Stowe put women, especially those who are mothers, at the very moral core of her opposition to slavery. The fact that families could be broken up and their members sold separately offended Stowe, as did that of their status as property and not people.

Many twentieth-century readers, especially beginning in the 1960s, have criticized the book for its disparaging image of Black people. The main character, Tom, for some, displays too much willingness to go along with his inferior status rather than fight it, giving rise to the pejorative term "Uncle Tom," meaning someone from the Black community complicit in or passive about slavery or Jim Crow laws and segregation. Yet others did not see Tom as self-effacing or passive, but rather as someone who stood up again and again to the abuse of his owners when it counted most. Indeed, Stowe intended the character to reflect a nobility of spirit implicit in her own Christian identity and to reflect, too, the fact that quite often in the slave-holding South the faith was shared by both masters and slaves. And while Stowe provides neither guidance nor inspiration for countering continued racism implicit in much of our modern national life, she does polemically emphasize the constitutional contradiction and religious anomaly of proverbially working both sides of the street. For some, the shared faith of Christians allowed them to temporize over the plight of slaves and put off ever doing anything to change

---

[90] Blight, *Frederick Douglass*, 247.

the status quo. But for significant numbers of others, it provided a constant goad to the conscience and a spur to speak out when it counted.

For our purposes, the Civil War gave ample opportunity for imagina-tions to flourish. How could America restore the Union and not just confine slavery but eliminate it altogether? After two years of conflict, it was time for action that would both speak to the moral strength of abolition itself and directly meet the strategic needs of Union forces engaged in varied fields of battle.

Although some advisors wanted Congress first to authorize abolition, Lincoln resolved to use the considerable power of the presidency to bring that much closer the reality of the promise of equal rights under law in the United States.

President Lincoln's Proclamation

> Now, therefore I, Abraham Lincoln, President of the United States, by virtue of the power in me vested as Commander-in-Chief, of the Army and Navy of the United States in time of actual armed rebel-lion against the authority and government of the United States, and as a fit and necessary war measure for suppressing said rebellion... *I do order and declare that all persons held as slaves within said designated States, and parts of States, are, and henceforward shall be free*; and that the Execu-tive government of the United States, including the military and naval authorities thereof, will recognize and maintain the freedom of said persons... [emphasis added].

> And upon this act, sincerely believed to be an act of justice, warranted by the Constitution, upon military necessity, I invoke the considerate judgment of mankind, and the gracious favor of Almighty God. In witness whereof, I have hereunto set my hand and caused the seal of the United States to be affixed.

By the President: ABRAHAM LINCOLN, September 22, 1862.

It remained for the Congress to ratify what the Proclamation had done and to expand its reach beyond the limited set of states covered in the proc-lamation to include all the others where slavery had been lawful. The Thir-teenth Amendment, proposed before the Southern states had been restored to the Union, should have easily passed the Congress. However, while the Senate passed it in April 1864, the House did not. At that point, Lincoln took an active role, insisting that its passage be added to the Republican

Party platform for the upcoming Presidential election. His efforts met with success, and the House passed the bill. On January 6, 1865, with a vote of 119–56, the amendment abolished slavery in the United States and provided that "[n]either slavery nor involuntary servitude, except as a punishment for crime whereof the party shall have been duly convicted, shall exist within the United States, or any place subject to their jurisdiction."

With its adoption, the United States found a final constitutional solution to the issue of slavery. The Thirteenth, Fourteenth, and Fifteenth Amendments make up a trio of Civil War amendments that greatly expanded the civil rights of Americans. All three had a bearing on the great moral contradiction of the American Constitution as first written and adopted. The Thirteenth Amendment had to affirm or formally authorize what Lincoln ordered with his Commander-in-Chief powers in the Emancipation Proclamation: to eradicate slavery from any and all territories of the country, including those not covered in the Proclamation as they were not under occupation by federal forces.

The Fourteenth Amendment, passed by Congress June 13, 1866, and ratified July 9, 1868, goes beyond fulfilling the promises of the constitutional showdown that the Civil War became, and it addresses the core ideas of due process and equal protection of the laws.

Another example of the revolutionary flavor of the Fourteenth Amendment rests with its specific reference to equality. Before the ratification of the Amendment in 1866, nowhere in the body of the original Constitution or even the Bill of Rights did the word "equality" appear. In all of our country's founding documents, only in the Declaration of Independence do we see the equality of human beings put forth as something we collectively believe in and support.

And though the Fifteenth Amendment the nation ensured that all formerly enslaved male citizens would not be disenfranchised on some other basis, such as racial identity or former condition of servitude, that guarantee continues, even into our present century, to need reinforcement by federal legislation. For many in the abolitionist movement, including both William Lloyd Garrison and Frederick Douglass, the adoption of the Fifteenth Amendment represented the capstone of their efforts. Douglass declared that the American Anti-Slavery Society had concluded its work.

As Section One declares:

> All persons born or naturalized in the United States and subject to the jurisdiction thereof, are citizens of the United States and of

the State wherein they reside. No State shall make or enforce any law which shall abridge the privileges or immunities of citizens of the United States; nor shall any State deprive any person of life, liberty, or property, without due process of law; nor deny to any person within its jurisdiction the equal protection of the laws.

First, recall that the first ten amendments, the original Bill of Rights, were written to assure the newly independent states that their citizens would not lose basic liberties to the new federal government. Nothing in those amendments addressed how, or whether, the courts of the land could enforce those rights or liberties against the states themselves.

Although the Fourteenth Amendment contains nothing explicitly on point, the Supreme Court has over the years held that such guarantees do indeed apply to the states. In a good modern example, the 1961 case of *Gideon v. Wainwright*, the Court decided that the concept of "ordered liberty," implicit in the term "due process," covers the right to counsel. By that judicial interpretation, then, the right to counsel carries over from the Sixth Amendment to the states, a right that has applied to federal court cases since the start of the Republic.

The legal development stemming from the Fourteenth Amendment has had a tremendous impact on how our federal system operates. By itself, this process of using amendments to blend or upgrade our liberties may well account for some historians' claims that the Civil War and its political consequences amounted to a second American Revolution.

Scarcely less important, the Fourteenth Amendment guarantees that the states must ensure *equal protection of the law* to all their citizens. That simple proposition alone has brought the ideal of equality down to earth in so much of our common civil life that we may not grasp how we would have functioned without it. Racial segregation in public schools might still exist had the Supreme Court, in the mid-twentieth century, not applied it in *Brown v. Board of Education*. The clause has prevented states from discriminating on racial grounds—and more recently on gender grounds—for marriage licenses. Not only do philosophers and historians address and debate the dynamic, fluid idea of equality, but so do judges and legislators. Indeed the ferment in that arena gives more than a modest laboratory for ideas that others of us have to think about as an ongoing enterprise. Consider, for example, the affirmative action policies still debated, still litigated, in college admissions. Or the overlap of rights in the freedom or liberty to form and practice religious beliefs when doing so affects access to services others need for their wellbeing. Discrimination as a legal complaint meets the claim of liberty more and more in the market place as it once did only in the realm of public administration.

Another example of the revolutionary flavor of the Fourteenth Amendment rests with its specific reference to equality. Before the ratification of the Amendment in 1866, nowhere in the body of the original Constitution, or even the Bill of Rights, did the word "equality" appear. In all of our country's founding documents, only in the Declaration of Independence do we see the equality of human beings put forth as something we collectively believe in and support.

For many in the abolitionist movement, including both William Lloyd Garrison and Frederick Douglass, the adoption of the Fifteenth Amendment represented the capstone of their efforts. Douglass declared that the American Anti-Slavery Society had concluded its work.

Not quite. The Constitution does not spell out the requirements for voting in elections for officers of the United States, for local or state offices. The states retain those. Thus, while the Fifteenth Amendment served a purpose, it prohibited only one kind disqualification for voting: "race, color, or previous condition of servitude."

Post-Reconstruction, following the adoption of the Amendment, it remained possible for southern states to require or continue to require a variety of other qualifications, including literacy, property ownership, and the poll tax, which proved formidable barriers to Black voting Indeed, those barriers remained effective all the way through the middle of the twentieth century.

CHAPTER SEVEN: RECONSTRUCTION

Although Reconstruction is widely described in history books as a failure, the notable Black historian of Reconstruction himself, W.E.B. Dubois, called it a "splendid failure" since it demonstrated the capacity of African Americans for the full enjoyment of citizens' rights.[91] And in the families, schools and churches of the time, it gave rise to the constitutional amendments that established the principle of legal and political equality regardless of race.

Before the War, Black men could vote only in a handful of states, and did not hold office—until Brownhelm Township, Ohio, made John N. Langston its town clerk in 1855. But during Reconstruction as many as two thousand African Americans held public office, from justice of the peace to governor. Thousands more headed Union Leagues and local branches of the Republican Party, edited newspapers, and in other ways influenced the political process,

Foner addresses the transformation of the region's politics, including the widespread interest among freedmen to absorb not only the news of the day but the country's history, in cities and in the "plantation belt" alike. Foner points to one White observer who noted that at gatherings like that in St. Landry, Louisiana, "several hundred freedmen gathered each Sunday at the offices of the local Republican newspaper to hear the weekly news read aloud."[92]

---

[91] W.E.B. Dubois, in *Forever Free: The Story of Emancipation and Reconstruction*, by Eric Foner, (New York: Vintage, 2006), xxvi.

[92] Eric Foner, *Reconstruction: America's Unfinished Revolution, 1863-1877*, (New York: Harper Modern Classics, 2014), 282.

While literacy presented a huge challenge, the majority of Black political leaders had learned to read and write secretly as slaves, in schools for free Blacks, in the Union army, or in institutions established after the war. Some of them—free before the war, especially in Virginia, South Carolina and Louisiana—possessed talents and training enough to become some of the most prominent Black officeholders in Reconstruction. Hiram Revels, born free in North Carolina, attended Knox College in Illinois, became a preacher, and later served as chaplain for a Black regiment during the war. After the war, he worked for the Freedmen's Bureau in Mississippi and, appointed to fill a vacant seat, became the first black man to serve in the U.S. Senate. Ironically, he filled the seat vacated when Jefferson Davis resigned to become leader of the Confederacy.

Did Blacks have sufficient votes to bring about these elections? In a word, no. Only in three states, South Carolina, Mississippi and Louisiana, did African Americans make up over half the population. In the other eight formerly Confederate states, the Republican Party needed the support of significant numbers of White male voters. Some—like Rufus Bullock, the first Republican governor of Georgia—saw the Party as the best chance for economic development of the region. Former president of the Macon and Augusta Railroad, and director of a bank, Bullock looked forward to an era when railroads, mines, machine shops and cotton mills financed by the North would supplant the plantation economy—concerns, that for Bullock, overshadowed race issues.

The un-wealthy White voters of the South who worked the land themselves without owning slaves did not welcome secession and the coming of the Confederacy. For many of these principally Upland southerners, the Republicans offered the opportunity to break the hold that the planter class had on state government and do a better job educating and serving the needs of laborers, White and Black.

Of course such sentiment came tinged with a racism all too familiar in other parts of the South, but the impulse for common cause could make a difference in how a White farmer might vote.

Down the road, the newly powerful South Carolina Republican party in its 1867 Convention called for an integrated public school system; protection against home seizure for debt; care for the aged and infirm; equal opportunity in public contracts; and heavy taxes on uncultivated land.

New constitutions won ratification in every state except Alabama, where a White boycott worked, and in Mississippi where a clause disenfranchising former Confederates alienated most White voters.

Schooling reflected the more general expansion of governmental activism and responsibility during Reconstruction. The creation of a tax-supported public school system in every state of the South stood as one of Reconstruction's most enduring accomplishments. By 1875, in states such as South Carolina and Mississippi, half the children of both races were attending public schools.[93]

Nearly all of these schools were racially segregated, though the new constitutions and laws did not require segregation, as they would post-Reconstruction. However, White parents largely refused to send their children with Black children.

Despite the shortcomings Reconstruction presented for the advance of equality, Foner maintains that "[g]rounded in the families, churches, schools and political institutions of the [B]lack community—the institutional infrastructure originating in slavery and consolidated after emancipation—former slaves continued to evince a powerful activism and exercised a considerable degree of political power." An experience worth celebrating, even while conceding that it did not last for long. An experience that demonstrates the power of solidarity and shared experience of adversity and oppression. And yet there remained plenty to lament including the resilience of local resistance and reaction; the unwillingness of Northern progressives to stay the course; and the stagnant material conditions of freedmen still at the economic mercy of their former owners. In that gap of larger restraining influence, the way was open for renewal of local oppression, this time beyond the confines of legitimate law enforcement.

The wave of counterrevolutionary terror that swept over large parts of the South between 1868 and 1871 lacks a counterpart either in the American experience or in that of the other Western Hemisphere societies that abolished slavery in the nineteenth century. Eric Foner has written and claims, too, that it is a "measure of how far change had progressed that the reaction against Reconstruction proved so extreme."[94]

Resistance to this extensive wave of violence, while scattered, sometimes proved effective. In 1868 the armed volunteer Union League managed to defy the Klan's effort to disrupt the vote on the state's new constitution in Wilmington, North Carolina. Congress, for its part, responded to the well-publicized hearings of 1870 and 1871 with three Enforcement Acts meant to suppress the violence. The most far-reaching KKK Act of 1871 became the first federal statute to punish acts by private individuals conspiring to

---

[93] Foner, *Reconstruction*, 170, 174.
[94] Foner, *Reconstruction*, 425.

deprive citizens of the right to vote. The Act further allowed the President to suspend the Writ of Habeas Corpus and use the army to enforce the law. Indeed, President Grant invoked the law soon after its passage. In South Carolina, he suspended the Writ in a number of upcountry counties; federal troops occupied the area and arrested an estimated two thousand Klansmen. Some dozen or so of the leaders were convicted and given prison terms. While the reign of terror ended, for the moment, by 1872 the sustained campaign of disruption had rattled the local organs of the Republican Party and the Union League, essentially returning Democrats to power in Tennessee and Georgia.

Persistent claims of corruption in the state governments of the Reconstruction South, often made but seldom authenticated, dovetailed with similar complaints about the Grant administration itself, especially during his second term. The climate of complaint led to a fatigue in federal leadership for any further civil rights efforts, especially after one of the strongest voices for continued reforms, Representative Charles Sumner of Pennsylvania, died in 1870. Then came the depression of 1873 and with it the unease of workers in the North. By the time Rutherford B. Hayes became the GOP candidate in 1876, the whole Reconstruction project was teetering on its last legs.

The essential lack of change in basic living and working conditions undermined the larger aims of Reconstruction. Land reform, as initially envisaged in the Freedmen's Bureau Act, never materialized. In a region dominated by agriculture and heavily dependent upon the cheapest possible labor, where would those freed workers gain a livelihood save on the very land they had cultivated as slaves? Despite a few exceptions, when freedmen could lease land for their own farming or, even more rarely, acquire it outright, most of the land abandoned by the Confederates did not get redistributed.

Perhaps the most visible legacy of the nation's experience of Civil War and Reconstruction are the two Great Migrations of Blacks from the South. The first, roughly 1915 to 1930, saw over one and a half million African Americans leave for cities of the Northeast and Midwest. The hardness of the Jim Crow era and the resurgence of White supremacy took the toll that the end of slavery alone did not bring about. The second lasting migration, from 1940–1970 and driven by the worst poverty in the Depression era of the 20th century, brought five million migrants out of the region.

While the end of slavery permitted, if not encouraged, Black movement out of the South, our national government could not, without more material support—particularly access to farmland—provide self-sufficiency for former slaves in the places of their birth. But the change in legal status delivered something of practical value—a passport to other parts of the nation, where they could find work and welcome.

The second way to look at these historic population shifts is thorough imperial projects in other times and settings. In the twentieth century, the British, the French, the Dutch, less so perhaps Spain and Portugal, gradually shrank or dismantled their overseas colonies and territories. As one consequence, a decades-long backflow of immigration from Africa, Asia, and the Americas ensued.

A very valuable insight about the relationship between historical interpretation and ongoing politics is brought to light by Eric Foner and in turn his reading of W.E.B. Du Bois's work. "The prevailing account of Reconstruction during the first half of the twentieth century formed an ideological pillar for the system of White supremacy. It provided justification for the White South's unalterable opposition to change in race relations and for decades of northern indifference to the nullification of the Fourteenth and Fifteenth Amendments."[95] The struggle for racial justice, Dubois believed, could not advance without a "corrected understanding of Reconstruction."[96]

It is Foner's claim that "two generations scholars have overturned virtually every assumption of the traditional viewpoint" and abandoned the racism at the base of that interpretation.[97]

---

[95] Eric Foner, *Forever Free: the Story of Emancipation and Reconstruction*, (New York: Vintage Books, 2006), xxvii.
[96] Foner, *Forever Free*, xxvii.
[97] Foner, *Forever Free*, xxvii.

Chapter Eight: Populism's Challenge to Exploitive Business

Under the new, post-Lincoln Republican Party, the nation let down its liberalizing burden of reconstruction with the 1876 election of Rutherford B. Hayes as president. In place of reconstruction the Republicans, conscious of their newly expanded popularity, eagerly took up the more inviting prospect of commercializing the vast interior of the country. The process, while underway before the War, got substantial boosts through large grants of land to railroad companies expanding across the plains. As Jill Lapore tells us, "Congress granted more than one hundred million acres of public lands in ten years."[98]

For a moment, back in the early days of the Civil War, the party of Lincoln had given an indication that something different could be in store for that region. In 1860, Congress defeated a bill to grant farm acreage to families willing to move there and enhance the land while making a living from it. Southern Democrats, fearing that anti-slavery sentiment would spread in the territories yet to be granted statehood, voted against the bill. Two years later, with the Southern representatives absent because of the war, Congress enacted the Homestead Act. It granted 160 acres to any head of household (without, Robert Fink tells us, a history of revolt against the Union[99]) who promised to farm the land for at least five years and pay a small registration fee. There would be no charge for the transfer of title. Thousands of the grantees were freedmen from the South, but many more might have quali-

---

[98] Jill Lapore, *These Truths, A History of the United States*, (New York: W.W. Norton, 2018), 333.

[99] Robert Fink, "Homestead Act of 1682," Britannica, https://www.britannica.com/topic/Homestead-Act.

fied had there been some financial support for equipment and supplies for farming, and home building. These costs were not large but consequential enough that many applicants went into commercial debt, despite the free land title.

Commercial banks became more prominent in the process. The railroads, too, turned to selling some of their new land to finance their own expansion and operation. As might be expected, the financial climate overheated; bankruptcies rose, but prices for railroad and bank stock fell fast. The New York Stock Exchange closed for ten days starting 20 September. By November 1873, some fifty-five of the nation's railroads had failed, and another sixty went bankrupt by the first anniversary of the crisis. Construction of new rail lines, formerly one of the backbones of the economy, plummeted from 7,500 miles of track in 1872 to just 1,600 miles in 1875. Eighteen thousand businesses failed between 1873 and 1875. Unemployment peaked in 1878 at 8.25%. Building construction was halted, wages were cut, real estate values fell and corporate profits vanished.[100]

"Go west, young man," advised Horace Greeley. Families heeded, and population in the region visibly expanded. "In 1870 only two million non-Indians lived west of the Missouri River but by 1890 that number had risen to more than ten million."[101] Farming families embodied the Jeffersonian ideal of independence and self-reliance. At the same time, financial challenges led many farmers to form cooperatives—the Grange in 1873, the National Farmers' Alliance in 1877—to build and operate grain storage facilities or collectively negotiate terms of freight rates for their harvests.

The reach of their economic power was blunted when the Supreme Court held their activities interfered with interstate commerce. Even so, the initiative of these farm-centered associations influenced the political rhetoric of the time. The more they called attention to the commercial power of banks and railroads over whole swaths of rural communities, the more state capitols would pay attention. By the time that one of their number from Omaha, Nebraska, began loudly complaining of the cost of borrowing money, a movement was well underway.

William Jennings Bryan (1860–1925) apparently had a voice that could command the attention of thousands at a time, indoors or out. No doubt he would have been comfortable using his powerful oratory from a pulpit, but his chosen mission was instead political. His ideas often used the vocabulary of Protestantism's Social Gospel, a term used to characterize Henry George's

---

[100] Lapore, *These Truths*, 335
[101] Lapore, 333.

invocation of evangelical zeal to advance an attack on economic inequality. The economic inequality of his time could be laid at the feet of the greed and avarice of those controlling wealth and the connivance of those running government. As a congressman, Bryan strongly supported a federal income tax with graduated rates. The one enacted to support the Union army and navy in the Civil War had expired, and another was not attempted again until 1894. It passed Congress but was overturned the next year by the Supreme Court as violative of the constitutional prohibition of direct taxes, a decision that William Howard Taft later disparaged as President when he actively supported adoption of the 16th Amendment.

Bryan would not see his goal fulfilled until the 1913 adoption of the Income Tax amendment, but it had continuous and broad support. By then, the term Gilded Age had entered the vocabulary and stood for the excesses in disparities of wealth not ever seen in America. It was not the case that reformers like Bryan or the People's Party had in mind an egalitarian plan of redistribution. The point was simply that the power and arrogance of the wealthy would not go unchallenged in America.[102] Republican Senator of Ohio John Sherman said of it: "the income tax is the only one that tends to equalize the burdens between rich and poor."[103]

Bryan's ambition led him to become a presidential contender, as a Democrat, three times—1896, 1900 and 1904—and he took the newly formed People's Party along with him. He carried "populism from the plains to the Potomac and turned the Democratic Party into the people's party," becoming "the first presidential candidate to campaign on behalf of the poor," as historian Jill Lapore has recently written.[104]

Economic inequality was central to serious politics, yet few plans emerged to address it systematically, despite frequent proposals for anti-monopoly laws and permanent income taxation. The larger intellectual task fell to an imaginative journalist named Henry George (1839–1897) who, in 1879, published his widely read book *Progress and Poverty: An Inquiry into the Causes of Industrial Depressions and Increase of Want with Increase of Wealth.* In it he focused on two central economic factors prominent in the Gilded Age. One was the paradox of great wealth and its accumulation existing alongside the widespread depression in the countryside as well as the cities. He

---

[102] In the 1895 Court decision in *Pollock v. Farmers' Loan and Trust Company*, one justice called the tax a first campaign in a "war of the poor against the rich."

[103] John Beatty, *Age of Betrayal: the Triumph of Money in America, 1865-1900,* (New York: Knopf, 2007), 200.

[104] Lapore, 345.

wanted to know how our country could produce so much wealth and at the same time see the benefits of that expansion so narrowly shared? The other phenomenon that George noticed was that wherever new investment took place, say, the extension of a rail line through new territory or space not fully developed, such as the edges of cities, there was a corresponding increase in the market value of that and adjacent land.

George decried the unevenness of benefits derived from technical innovation and discovery.[105] Financial capitalism, George argued, was "destroying democracy by making economic equality impossible."[106] Land ownership, George saw, was powerfully connected to accumulation of wealth, so he felt we should tax its rental value as a resource common to all citizens and not the labor of making it productive, whether by tenant farmers or factory wage earners. As the rental value increases over time, he argued, as it would from private investment in a factory, for example, or through public investment in roads, bridges, schools and so on, there would be enough revenue to replace other more conventional taxes on sales and income.

What crippled the egalitarian impetus of the populists, as it would many progressives later, was the undisguised racism or indifference to the former slaves as a group. Support for the cause of women's suffrage, on the other hand, was at least voiced by Bryan and others; but they offered no words about the injustices of the Jim Crow regime of forced segregation in the states of the former Confederacy. Neither President Theodore Roosevelt nor his Democratic successor—Woodrow Wilson- challenged the status quo. "In an angry White House encounter with the black leader William Monroe Trotter in 1914, Wilson finally admitted what was obvious: that he believed segregation was the best policy for African-Americans."[107]

Of the three presidents allied with Progressivism—Roosevelt, Taft and Wilson—it was the third, and the only one of them elected as a Democrat, who, as a matter of his administration's policy, pushed the federal government further away from racial equality than anyone else. Wilson, in April 1913, the first year of his administration, imposed racial segregation through department after department.[108]

Distinctive voices of protest from the Black community kept the issue alive through a long period of hostility or indifference toward civil rights.

---

[105] On the very dawn of the Industrial Revolution Jean Jacques Rousseau made much the same claim in his first published essay, discussed in Chapter One.

[106] Lapore, 342.

[107] Michael McGerr, *A Fierce Discontent: The Rise and Fall of the Progressive Movement in America*, (Oxford: Oxford University Press, 2003), 196.

[108] Lapore, *These Truths*, 389.

One of these was Ida Wells (1862–1931), a school teacher from Mississippi and daughter of former slaves who, in 1892, published *Southern Horrors, Lynch Law in all its Phases*. After her newspaper's Memphis office was destroyed by arson in the 1880s, she elected to move to New York City to continue her work by witness and writing. And so did another well-known reformer from the South, W.E.B. Du Bois (1868–1963). A college professor in Atlanta, he had developed the social survey as an instrument not merely for scholarship but also for effective journalism. In 1909, Du Bois, along with several White supporters, formed the National Association for the Advancement of Colored People to inform, educate and litigate. The legal wing of the organization chalked up its earliest judicial win in Oklahoma when they persuaded the court that a state law grandfathering voters from the rolls of 1866 was unconstitutional. The statute's cut-off date was of course designed to re-enfranchise any former confederates in the state and to discourage or deny voting by former slaves given the vote by the Fifteenth Amendment.

By the last decade of the nineteenth century, very little had been done to challenge the high rate of income inequality in the age of big business, although the rhetoric for reform was considerable. The deepening social divide of the races, on the other hand, was challenged even less. The pervasiveness of the Jim Crow regime in the South led to the growth in other regions of practices promoting segregation, but without the formality of ordinance or statute. Restrictive covenants in deeds used in real estate developments became a significant element of what came to be called "de facto" segregation that endured just as long as, if not longer than, the *de jure* kind of the Jim Crow South.

It is impossible to know, of course, how the spread and depth of racial segregation might have been challenged earlier than it was, well into America's twentieth century. Near the end of the nineteenth century, however, the Supreme Court of the United States gave the policy of racial division enough official legitimacy to make its overthrow that much more difficult and its continuity prolonged.

In 1897, the Supreme Court decided 8–1 that a state was free to insist on separate train cars for passengers of different races. At issue in *Plessy v. Ferguson* (1896) was whether the statute violated the Fourteenth Amendment's equal protection clause. "Separate" did not imply *unequal* treatment in and of itself, the Court reasoned. That concept "separate but equal" would come to underpin a broad regime of racial segregation—"colored" separate from "white"—not only in trains and buses but also hotels, restaurants, movie theaters, and more. Even court houses would have separate water fountains, rest rooms and seating areas. The most telling impact of this decision would have to be in the public schools. The impressionable members of each succeeding generation would grow up knowing only a segregated social life.

In his 2003 book, *A Fierce Discontent: The Rise and Fall of the Progressive Movement in America*, historian Michael McGerr devotes a whole chapter to "the Shield of Segregation" behind which otherwise reform-minded leaders would constantly defer to a seemingly immutable social reality (182–218). Progressives, McGerr claims, knew well enough that segregation did not separate equals from one another, "one party always ended up with less— less power, less wealth, less opportunity, less schooling, less health care, less respect."[109] Their choice not to confront segregation, McGerr believes, was in deference to the primacy of their efforts against economic inequality among classes of Americans.[110] Improvement in racial division and inequality would "take longer" was the default attitude of the sympathetic Progressives. As Lapore points out, when Progressives—and Populists before them—"talked about inequality they meant the condition of White farmers and White wage earners relative to business owners," but nonetheless they "were undeniably influenced by the struggle for racial justice," in particular by the investigative journalism pioneered by Ida B. Wells, for example.[111]

One might be forgiven in thinking of populist and progressive indifference to segregation as correlated to the nativist farm culture of their base. As a politician of the Plains, William Jennings Bryan steered clear of the pervasive spread of segregation and focused on economic inequality and the power of railroads and banks dominating so much of the life in small towns and farms of the Midwest. Nor did the idealist journalist Henry George build racial division into his theory. While his focus on the built-in bias in favor of land ownership and the capital formation it promoted could well have been demonstrated among Black owners, George did not himself make the connection.

The president who best exemplifies the Progressive Movement (1890–1920) and its reach into actual political and legal reform, Theodore Roosevelt, used his platform to fight the pervasive influence of big business. While at the height of his rhetorical form, he slammed the controllers of Wall Street and their trusts, dusted off the Sherman Act of 1894, and began prosecuting. In 1901, the first year of his presidency, he used that law to break up a combi-

---

[109] McGerr, *Fierce Discontent*, 183.
[110] McGerr, 183.
[111] Lapore, 371.

nation of railroads in the Northwest. More famously, in 1906, he used it to break up the cartel of the biggest producers of oil under the Rockefellers— Standard Oil Company.

Roosevelt, certainly no enemy of capitalism, believed that the promise of prosperity had to go beyond profits for the companies dominating the markets in various sectors. The principal evil of "bigness" lay in its tendency to restrict or dampen competition and thus keep the prices of commodities and services at abnormally high rates. So, to that extent Roosevelt, with his embrace of the anti-trust instrument of government regulation, earned the gratitude of voters both rural and urban, and the enmity of many from his own party.

Chapter Nine: The Urban Soul of Progressivism

If the political face of the Progressive Era took on the image of Theodore Roosevelt and his robust assault on the bigness of business, then the mind and heart belong to Jane Addams (1860–1935). More than any other single individual, man or woman, she embodied—and wrote about—what it meant to live and work in the midst of the city dwellers who paid much of the human cost in America's experience of industrialization.

Among many other distinctions, Addams virtually invented a new profession—Social Work—to confront that milieu. She used Settlement House in White Chapel of East London as a blueprint for the founding and operation of Hull House in Chicago in the late 1880s, an idea and practice that spread quickly across the country and eventually emerged as an all-purpose community center like that in many of American cities of a much later time. Established for families of very limited resources or opportunities, the centers provided an array of services: day care for working mothers; literacy training, especially for immigrant families; as well as classes in learning to cope with the rules of the city—or the absence of many municipal services we take for granted, like trash collection, water service, or electricity.

The example of White Chapel in East London borrowed by Jane Addams and others had implications far broader than that of volunteer-staffed social assistance. The cities of both Europe and America in the late nineteenth century had had no official systematic support or subsidy for any purpose, save for state highways passing through their boundaries—they were on their own to finance improvements of all kinds. The attention they needed and eventually got during the Progressive Age came from each city itself.

Early impressive examples included Berlin, Birmingham, and Glasgow, later followed by Toronto, New York, and Chicago.

Population growth fed by the vigor of commerce was not met with plans for housing growth, or other kinds of planning. The realm of city life was replete with privatization to the point of gridlock. Cities, Daniel Rogers tells us, "swarmed with commercial water suppliers, carters, private refuse haulers and street sweeping contractors and streetcar companies."[112] Where capital investment of a higher order was called for, as in street car and gas systems, the applicant company would frequently succeed in acquiring a monopoly of that service.[113] One can imagine that the situation was not free from bribery or other forms of corruption.

How did cities ever gain control of their nominal ownership and operation of such services? Perhaps it was just pragmatic, a recognition of the unseemliness of the city as fighting turf for numerous competitors. The examples of European cites was also important. The progressives among the business class in American cities eventually "engineered a major shift in the line between city and private enterprise...[and] collective tasks" grew first out of public health concerns, which led to American cities investing heavily in public water and sewer facilities.[114] Roads and streetcars were more expensive to improve because U.S. cities typically had more territory than European ones. America led the way in building public schools—though often too few, which resulted in overcrowding—as well as in establishing parks and playgrounds, many of which found favor among European visitors. Olmstead's Central Park in NYC from the 1850s, for example, set the pace.

Urban progressives managed to build alliances across classes and thus illustrated how strengthened municipal services benefited the diverse neighborhoods of a city. In bringing cultural amenities to "the slums," for example, twentieth-century sociologist Lewis Mumford suggests, in *The Culture of Cities*, that the Settlement House called attention also to the insufficiency of civic awareness in affluent neighborhoods as well.[115]

Several features of Addams's work concretely reflect the idea of equality—as in mutual respect and solidarity. Settlement House—the phrase refers to the residents themselves who paid their own room and board and considered themselves "settlers" in the neighborhood—established a symbiotic

---

[112] Daniel T. Rogers, *Atlantic Crossings: Social Politics in a Progressive Age*, (Cambridge: The Belknap Press of Harvard University Press, 1998), 116.

[113] Rogers, *Atlantic Crossings*, 118.

[114] Rogers, 130-31

[115] Lewis Mumford, *The Culture or Cities*, (New York: Harcourt, Brace and Company, 1938), 298.

relationship between inhabitants of the house and the community. Addams did not consider the volunteer hours put in by affluent, socially-conscious community members charity work, especially because the early residents at Hull House, typically immigrants, wanted to learn from their neighbors—not just English, but also about the culture, law and politics of their new community.

The home welcomed both men and women, installing them on separate floors but otherwise on equal terms. The presence of women among the settlers critically helped win the trust of the mothers and other women of the neighborhood. Just as importantly, Addams needed male community volunteers to demonstrate a cooperative example for immigrant men accustomed to different gender roles in their cultures of origin.

On occasion, Addams and her associates (often drawn from numbers of college or graduate students seeking practical experience and empirical studies for their academic work) engaged political leaders on issues that especially impacted their neighbors. In particular, working hours for women and children profoundly impacted health and education. Although Addams tried to remain officially independent of labor unions, she wanted to support them, and allowed them to use Hull House for member meetings. Likewise she made sure Hull House declined endorsement or sponsorship by any church or other religious entity lest they alienate some neighbors.

In the wake of founding of Hull House—a place that spawned a movement—Jane Addams became a prominent figure in national politics. In 1912 she spoke to the Progressive National Convention, nominating Teddy Roosevelt as their candidate for president. It is a mark not just of her own accomplishments but also how far the Progressive cause had advanced over the course of two decades. Addams called attention to the ways in which her country seemed to have fallen behind the social advances made in other countries; despite its Gilded Age, the United States remained sluggish in coming to terms with its consequences, or as Rogers puts it, "[t]he new party has become the American exponent of a world-wide movement toward [more just] social conditions, a movement which the United States, lagging behind other great nations, has been unaccountably slow to embody in political action."[116] Richard Hofstadter, in *Anti-intellectualism in American Life*, remarks that

> [t]he country seems to have been affected by a sort of spiritual hunger, a yearning to apply to social problems the principles of Chris-

---

[116] Rogers, 74-5.

tian morality which has always characterized its creed but too rarely its behavior. It felt a greater need for self-criticism and self-analysis. The principles of good government that the gentlemen reformers had called for in vain seemed to be closer to realization.[117]

Going beyond the reach of municipal governance, the time was ripe for addressing issues that called for more comprehensive, national reforms. A high priority was the protection of industrial workers, their job sites and health support. Addams found a fairly complete list of needed reforms in the program a notable European leader had hammered out for his country a generation before.

Otto Bismarck, a Prussian oligarch with his own legacy as a German hero, had a clear vision. He saw a unified German nation strong enough to exert influence on all its near neighbors, to keep the peace, and to reward its citizens with the advantages of industrial, financial and commercial prosperity.

Ironically, Bismarck—as the strong, centralizing leader of Germany in its full economic and political maturity—presided over the first welfare state. He led Germany to adopt a range of measures to secure more advantages for those working in the factories, mills and mines than the English, French, or Americans would see for another generation. In brief, the major components of this earliest version of the Welfare State included Workers' Compensation for industrial accidents; limitations on hours of work; prohibitions of child labor; rights to organize unions and collective bargaining with industry; old age pensions; and medical insurance funds for workers and their families. All of these came to their first systematic expression in an industrial powerhouse led by a man no one has ever called a progressive.[118] Bismarck brilliantly invested his ambition to build a strong state with a strategy to solidify working class loyalty toward the state and thereby blunt the appeal of socialism and the unions as competitors.

Addams's address to fellow Progressives in 1912 reflected a marked conservative strand of thought prevalent in her era. A principal indication was the Supreme Court case of *Lochner v. New York*, decided in 1905. The state legislature had passed a statute limiting the number of hours permitted in bakeries to ten hours per day and sixty hours per week. The industry challenged that the law interfered with the liberty of contract guaranteed to bakery owners by the due process clause of the Fourteenth Amendment.

---

[117] Richard Hofstadter, *Anti-Intellectualism in American Life*, (New York: Alfred A. Knopf, 1969), 197.

[118] See Daniel T. Rogers, *Atlantic Crossings* (1998); Jill Lapore, *These Truths* (2018); and Michael McGerr, *A Fierce Discontent* (2013).

In a divided opinion, the Court endorsed the challenge and at once cast a pall over labor law reforms for thirty years. Law Professor Lawrence Tribe acknowledges the wide legislative and judicial "resistance to the Progressive movement" and that the Court's views "echoed a powerful strand in the thought and politics of the early twentieth century."[119]

Such issues would not come to a turning point in the political arena for decades. In that interval, however, Addams and hosts of her colleagues would unleash a parallel energy on other unfinished work of progressives—suffrage for women.

---

[119] Lawrence Tribe, *American Constitutional Law*, (New York: Foundation Press, 1978), 435. In his dissenting opinion Justice Oliver Wendell Holmes labeled the decision as carrying social Darwinism into the Constitution and he specifically decried the ideas of Herbert Spencer. See Chapter Five.

Chapter Ten: The Citizenship of Women

Long before the singular, national expression of political equality for women, several states already guaranteed the franchise, the right to vote. Most notably, Wyoming and Montana included such a provision in their founding constitutions. And while not a new idea for America, nationwide recognition took so long that the Nineteenth Amendment—"The right of citizens of the United States to vote shall not be denied or abridged by the United States or by any State on account of sex. Congress shall have power to enforce this article by appropriate legislation"—seems oddly misplaced in the twentieth century. It truly belongs to the mid-1800s with the confluence of ideas and events which brought the United States its "second Revolution" with the Civil War, constitutional amendments, and Reconstruction. And yet, not until the twentieth century, one hundred and forty years after the nation's founding did the moment crystallize. The course of that long political evolution itself speaks of major imperatives and not a few stalwart seekers along its path way.[120]

Why did the project to liberate women from the unique bondage of condescension and exploitation take so long? One answer might be the sheer inertia at large of being taken for granted, put off, and kept "in their place."[121] Despite the tenacious efforts of women and men for equal rights for women, the indifferent silence of so many others proved stronger.

---

[120] *The Woman's Hour* by Elaine Weiss (2019) is the most comprehensive study of the Right to Vote movement in the United States including details about ratification in the states. Tennessee's legislative vote in 1919 was the crucial one.

[121] John Ralston Saul, *The Unconscious Civilization*, (New York: Free Press, 1995) 162.

What seems to have been missing for so long was a movement, the formation of organizations avowedly devoted to the goal of enfranchisement over a sustained period of time.[122] In such movements there is often more than one relevant organization and more than one notable leader. In the movement to enfranchise American women there were indeed multiple organizations and more than one significant leader at work. Elizabeth Cady Stanton (1815–1902) was not only a powerful voice for women's political rights but she was also concerned with inequalities between the sexes more generally. While notable men in public life—writers like J.S. Mill, George Bernard Shaw, even President Woodrow Wilson—spoke out in their times, they did not form a movement. In 1901, at a New York City Jewish girls' school, Samuel Clemens —"Mark Twain"—gave a prescient speech supporting equal voting rights for women, predicting that the cause would succeed within twenty-five years, which it in fact did.

Yet the story of success in achieving the right to vote belongs by and large to women themselves, and to their ability to organize for collective action. Some of their leaders' names—like Susan B. Anthony—have become synonymous with courage, energy and vision. Although less frequently remembered in the popular press than Anthony, Elizabeth Cady Stanton (1815–1902) warrants singular focus in this account. In 1868, Stanton boldly addressed the Women's Suffrage Convention:

> I urge a sixteenth amendment, because "manhood suffrage," or a man's government, is civil, religious, and social disorganization. The male element is a destructive force, stern, selfish, aggrandizing, loving war, violence, conquest, acquisition, breeding in the material and moral world alike discord, disorder, disease, and death. See what a record of blood and cruelty the pages of history reveal![123]

Stanton's blunt assessment barely disguises her bitterness at having lost the effort to persuade Congress to include women's right to vote in the Fifteenth Amendment. She must have been equally disappointed by Abolitionist movement ally, Frederick Douglass, who did not support the inclusion. She and Anthony broke with him and others, and lobbied against both the Fourteenth and Fifteenth Amendments without provision for women to

---

[122] Not unlike the large scale movements we call revolutions reviewed in Chapter Two. And not unlike the co-op movement launched by Robert Owen of the early 1800s and briefly described in Chapter Four. The Quakers, too, working continually in that century against the slave trade, make the same point.

[123] Elizabeth Cady Stanton. "The Destructive Male." Great Speeches Collection. *The History Place.* http://www.historyplace.com/speeches/stanton.htm.

vote. They feared that by enfranchising only males from the population of former slaves, the number of voters willing to deny women their place in the civic order would only increase. All women and men of both races should advance together, they argued. "The prejudice against color…is no stronger than that against sex. It is produced by the same cause and manifested in the same way," Stanton wrote.

Twenty years before she made that speech, Elizabeth Stanton demonstrated her strong leadership abilities and her social imperatives at The Seneca Falls Convention of 1848—the earliest large scale expression for women's rights in the United States. With the help of Susan B. Anthony she organized and welcomed more than three hundred people from across the country. Stanton read her "Declaration of Sentiments" on the first day of the meeting, and invited the general public in for discussion of particular proposals on the second. Surprisingly, the initial call for the right to vote did not have anywhere near unanimous backing, but Frederick Douglass, in attendance at the debate, lent his vocal support, and the measure passed.

The town of Seneca Falls still celebrates the recognition from the Convention that spawned annual gatherings in larger cities all over the Eastern Seaboard until decades later when the country entered into World War I. After meeting in 1852, Stanton and Anthony went on to found, in 1866, the National Association for Women's Suffrage (NAWS)—the principal expression of women's rights promotion for two generations. Stanton's feminist concerns, broader than Anthony's, covered the gamut: divorce laws, birth control, parental custody, property rights, and access to employment and the professions. Additionally, Stanton's views on religion sometimes made her more controversial than was good for the cause. Despite their differences, Stanton and Anthony remained allies. Whereas Anthony, who never married, Stanton (both wife and mother of seven) wanted to address inequities in the laws governing property and family relations as well.

Prior to living in Seneca Falls, Stanton had become an admirer and friend of Lucretia Mott, the Quaker minister, feminist, and abolitionist. They met at the World Anti-Slavery Convention in London, England, during Stanton's honeymoon in the spring of 1840. The two women became allies when the male delegates attending the convention voted to prohibit women's participation in the proceedings, even if they, like Mott, served as official delegates of their respective abolitionist societies. After considerable debate, a compromise required women to sit in a roped-off section hidden from the men in attendance. William Lloyd Garrison, the prominent American abolitionist, arrived after the vote, refused his seat in protest, electing instead to sit with the women. The decision to prohibit women from participating in the convention strengthened Stanton's commitment to women's rights. By 1848, her early life experiences, together with the experience in London and her initially isolating experience as a housewife in Seneca Falls, galvanized Stanton:

> The general discontent I felt with woman's portion as wife, housekeeper, physician, and spiritual guide, the chaotic conditions into which everything fell without her constant supervision, and the wearied, anxious look of the majority of women, impressed me with a strong feeling that some active measures should be taken to remedy the wrongs of society in general, and of women in particular. My experience at the World Anti-slavery Convention, all I had read of the legal status of women, and the oppression I saw everywhere, together swept across my soul, intensified now by many personal experiences. It seemed as if all the elements had conspired to impel me to some onward step. I could not see what to do or where to begin—my only thought was a public meeting for protest and discussion.[124]

Stanton's frustrations with the abolitionist movement may have helped her, and others like Anthony, connect to their own experience of discrimination and dependence more deeply. They saw, among other social deprivations in their status, the pervasive abuse of alcohol by men—husbands and fathers. The social problem deserved attention, and became their principal cause through Women's Temperance Unions, until they acknowledged they needed the vote to convince politicians that the cause had merit. Elizabeth Stanton shifted her energy and understanding that if she—and women like her—did not have equal footing as a member of the political community, her voice would be forever diminished if not dismissed outright.

Stanton's strength of character and mind was evident from her youth. Although not intellectually encouraged by her father, Stanton won Latin prizes in school and, from a teacher who lived next door to her family home, learned Greek and borrowed his books. Her willingness to accept help where and from whom she could became a keystone of her leadership. Although she apparently lived a satisfying family life, whenever asked about it, she made clear her husband did not support women's right to vote. She carried on without it. As far as we know, the only thing she asked of him as a public person—he was one of the co-founders of the Republican Party—was that he put the suffrage proposals before their state legislature.

---

[124] Elizabeth Cady Stanton, *Eighty Years & More: Reminiscences 1814-1897* (London: T. Fisher Unwin,1998), 148.

Meanwhile an equally potent movement was taking place in Edwardian England. Emmeline Pankhurst (1858–1928), the British equivalent of Elizabeth Stanton, just as steadfastly championed women's right to vote. They overlapped in life and mission though almost two generations apart in age. Pankhurst, too, rejected the scourge of slavery in America, after her mother read *Uncle Tom's Cabin* to her and her siblings. She became an avid reader and found much inspiration in Thomas Carlyle's *History of the French Revolution*— so much so that as an adult she intentionally recorded her own birth date one day earlier, so that she could count the fall of the Bastille as symbolic of her own commitments for reform in Britain.[125]

While both were fully committed to equal political rights for women, Stanton and Pankhurst used different tactics. Pankhurst, adopted a more robust activism and helped found a more avowedly political group named the Women's Social and Political Union (WSPU) in 1906. The organization elected to go beyond words and combine their voices with deeds—or, some would say, vandalism—to trespass with their placards and interrupt events. Pankhurst and others went to jail several times in that period, raising both dissension within the ranks of the reformers and disparagement from the public at large. During World War I the WSPU deliberately called a halt to their militancy and favored the government's pursuit of war with Germany. This proved as controversial within the voting rights community as the militancy of the WSPU had been in the public at large. But, by the time of the 1918 Armistice and the return of peace, Parliament acted to change the law. A coalition government passed the Representation of the People Act which gave the vote to all men, regardless of property holding, and to women over the age of thirty. In 1928 Parliament, repealed the age distinction; women and men could now vote, on equal terms, from the age of twenty-one.

Historic Antecedents

Having explored in Chapter Two the signal document of the French Revolution—The Declaration of the Rights of Man (1789)—one might expect to find in it something explicit about women's rights, specifically political ones. But no, as Simon Schama reports, "having created an all-embracing concept of citizenship," the National Assembly "subsequently decided that some

---

[125] Carlyle's assessment of the French Revolution was critical not of the agents of change and their sources of inspiration, like Rousseau, as is Edmund Burke's earlier account, but on the nobility and monarchists who provoked it. They clung to their privileges over long through their abuse of them. See Chapter Three.

were more equal than others" and limited voting participation to males—of certain status and age—only.[126]

That was not the end of the matter, however. A number of voices, both male and female, rose in protest. Probably the most enduring of those belonged to well-known dramatist, Olympe de Gouges, who in 1791 published her famous *Declaration of the Rights of Women and Citizens*. Not disguising her satirical intent, Gouges composed her book in the same number of articles as the Declaration of the Rights of Man. The first article declared "woman is born free and lives equal to man in her rights" and the second that "the purpose of any political association is the conservation of the natural and imprescriptible rights of woman and man."[127]

Two other important names and one of their initiatives illustrate the vibrancy of the time. The Marquis de Condorcet (1743–1794) and his wife Sophie (1758–1822), while born into aristocratic families, both embraced the democratic ideals of the Revolution. Working as colleagues, they determined to see those goals promoted through informed writing in a journal open to wide subscription. They inspired and participated in numerous public meetings in provincial cities as well as Paris. Keenly aware of substantial opposition to their reformist views, the Marquis and Sophie Condorcet sought to have the broadest possible reach. Political clubs were spawned in the process. This *Cercle Social*—The Social Circle, or Society of the Friends of Truth—prepared the ground for what Jonathan Israel calls a "politically organized feminism that conquered a narrow but real enclave in the public sphere ... forged for the first time in human history."[128] Through such efforts, by 1792 the National Assembly not only instituted divorce for the first time in French history and on equal grounds, it also decreed that children of both sexes would inherit equally and declared that adult children would no longer be subject to parental control. "In short," Lynn Hunt summarizes in *Inventing Human Rights*, "the revolutionaries did everything they could to push out the boundaries of personal autonomy."[129]

Yet the summit of revolutionary support for full women's rights—voting membership in French society—remained out of reach until the modern era. The Marquis, himself "the most outspoken male defender of the political rights of women during the Revolution,"[130] offered his own take on the

---

[126] Schama, 489.
[127] Israel, *Revolutionary Ideas*, 125.
[128] Israel, 125.
[129] Hunt, 62.
[130] Hunt, 169.

weight of social custom: "Habit can familiarize men with the violation of their natural rights to the point that among those who have lost them no one dreams of reclaiming them or believes that he has suffered an injustice."[131]

The long, long journey for women's right to vote underscores something important about a struggle waged largely through ideas in print. In fact, before the publication by an English woman in 1792, the "concept of women's rights got virtually no hearing in England or America."[132] Mary Wollstonecraft, whose first book in defense of the French Revolution we discussed in Chapter Three, added her voice with the publication of her second book in 1792. *Vindication of the Rights of Woman*, Christine Stansell suggests, "laid the intellectual basis for modern feminism."[133] While that tradition smoldered for a century, and critics sought to disparage her ideas by slighting her personal life, Wollstonecraft's "achievement was to announce, in a hundred different ways...that power, not nature, determined the relations of women and men. Expectations about how women should think and act were in truth born of a system of male privilege and tyranny as corrupt as any monarchy."[134]

Provoked by a proposal for a national program of education in France, Wollstonecraft used her second book to express particular concern with the education of girls, finding it, as traditionally practiced, inadequate to prepare them as women for the full array of rights and responsibilities of citizenship as envisioned in the Declaration of the Rights of Man. She even included an open letter to Charles-Maurice de Talleyrand, the French education minister, urging him to reconsider the pending proposal with its two-track system wherein girls would stop with books and classrooms at age of eight and be assigned to their respective homes for training in customary domestic skills. Her text clearly reflects the naturalistic approach to childhood education she had found appealing in Rousseau's writings, especially his novel *Emile*. Wollstonecraft also clearly rejected the view implicitly held by both Rousseau and Talleyrand that differences in the nature of the two sexes determined the difference in educational policy.[135]

---

[131] Hunt, 170. How familiar this attribute of conventional opinion must have seemed to Elizabeth Stanton in 1860s America as she carried on with her project after being rebuffed in the drafting of the Fifteenth Amendment by a former ally Frederick Douglass fearful of rejection by male voters had women been included

[132] Hunt, 172.

[133] Christine Stansell, *The Feminist Promise, 1792 to the Present*, (New York: Modern Library, 2011), 25.

[134] Stansell, *Feminist Promise*, 25-6.

[135] See Alice S. Rossi, *The Feminist Papers, From Addams to de Beauvoir*, (Boston: Northeastern University Press), 31-2. This book contains a brisk biography of Wollstonecraft as well as the full text of her second book.

A Boost from Outside the Circle of Women

Earlier we identified John Stuart Mill as the "apostle of individualism" and emphasized the influence his most notable book, *On Liberty* (1859), has had for political theory through his century and the next. Here Mill re-emerges with specific resonance because of another of his books, this one perhaps not so widely read, *The Subjection of Women* (1869). In its time, this book was singularly important for those seeking to advance the equality of women. Elizabeth Stanton, according to Stansell, "revered Mill and used his ideas to hone her own."[136] Mill makes three coordinated main arguments in this powerful essay.[137]

One. Nothing other than tyranny exercised by males, both by custom and even sanctioned by Christianity, keeps women from being free to pursue their own happiness as fully as men. The rule of force has been abandoned or overthrown in modern times in the case of chattel slavery, but for women it persists both as a legal imposition in the status of wife, and in the public domain where women are deprived of responsible employment and of the right to vote. Mill asks and answers, "[f]or what is the peculiar character of the modern world—the difference which chiefly distinguishes modern institutions, modern social ideas, modern life itself, from those of times long past? It is that human beings are no longer born to their place in life and chained down by an inexorable bond."[138]

Two. The world is a poorer place because of the subjection of women. One half the world's population is being denied access to education and other fulfillment of its natural capacities. In every sphere of human endeavor including sciences, literature, public leadership, the professions there would be advances in our civilization denied under these ancient customs and laws.

Three. Perhaps the most telling of Mill's arguments is a psychological one. Men do not want solely the obedience of women, they want their sentiments...The masters of women wanted more than obedience, and they turned

---

[136] Stansell, 94.

[137] The customary attribution of authorship to Mill has not been a particular concern of those like Stanton who learned from it and were inspired by the book. Yet there are recurring comments about how the long collaboration between Mill and Harriet Taylor, first as friends, then as a married couple, likely impacted the work. Richard Reeves's *John Stuart Mill: Victorian Firebrand* examines their collaboration exhaustively. Alice Rossi in her *The Feminist Papers* believes that *The Subjection* would not have been begun "without Harriet's role in Mill's personal and intellectual life" (183). Christine Stansell, in *The Feminine Promise*, making a point about "germinative relationships" among writers on feminism, notes that Mill's book was "heavily indebted to Harriet Taylor" (75).

[138] John Stuart Mill, *The Subjection of Women*, (Fairhope: Mockingbird, 2015), 19.

the whole force of education to effect their purpose. All women are brought up from the earliest years in the belief that their ideal of character is the very opposite to that of men: not self-will and government by self-control, but submission and yielding to the control of others.[139]

And that's not the worst of it, for men have made themselves into selfish exploiters of this power over women, "by representing to them meekness, submissiveness and resignation of all individual will into the hands of a man as an essential part of sexual attractiveness"[140]

Mill recognized these among other indicators of women's subordination: (1) British women had fewer grounds for divorce than men (until 1923); (2) husbands controlled their wives' personal property until the Married Women's Property Acts of 1870 and 1882; (3) children belonged to the husbands; (4) rape was impossible within a marriage; and (5) wives lacked crucial features of legal personhood, because the husband stood as the representative of the family, thereby eliminating the need for women's suffrage.

Not only were these disabilities wrong in themselves for denying a woman's individuality, but also they also stunted the moral development of both women and men. Women learned to be submissive or became bitterly isolated, neglecting their own talents and intellect. And men often developed the habits of brutishness in the power they had over their wives. A shared "perfect equality," among *women*, men, and their families would result in a healthier society, benefited by the contributions of all its members.

Mill remains relevant well into the twenty-first century. Christine Stansell maintains that even for women of the twentieth century

> ...who have seen very little difference in the actual condition, if not the formal rights, of women under any form of government—whether Fascist, Communist or Democratic—*The Subjection of Women* continues to serve as a resounding affirmation of their human right to full equality and a sophisticated analysis of the obstacles that bar their way to it.[141]

The final formality of the vote for women was a phenomenon of the twentieth century, as we have seen in 1920 America and 1928 Britain. For other countries it happened a bit later, mostly in the 1940s.[142]

---

[139] Mill, *Subjection*, 20.

[140] Mill, *Subjection*, 20.

[141] Stansell, 194.

[142] France, for example, emerging from the German occupation of World War II, gave women the vote in 1944. For the world at large after that war, as we will see in Chapter Eleven, a fitting capstone was set in place as part of the Universal Declaration of Human Rights in 1948. The former First Lady of the country during the Great Depression and World War II represented the United States in negotiating the treaty signed in Paris

Relevant Parts of the Preamble and the Wording of Article 21:

Preamble

Whereas recognition of the inherent dignity and of the equal and inalien-able rights of all members of the human family is the foundation of freedom, justice and peace in the world,

...

Whereas the peoples of the United Nations have in the Charter reaf-firmed their faith in fundamental human rights, in the dignity and worth of the human person and in the equal rights of men and women and have determined to promote social progress and better standards of life in larger freedom...

Article 21

(1) Everyone has the right to take part in the government of his country, directly or through freely chosen representatives.

(2) Everyone has the right of equal access to public service in his country.

(3) The will of the people shall be the basis of the authority of govern-ment; this will shall be expressed in periodic and genuine elections which shall be by universal and equal suffrage and shall be held by secret vote or by equivalent free voting procedures.

in 1948. See Mary Ann Glendon, *A World Made New: Eleanor Roosevelt and the Universal Declaration of Human Rights* (New York: Random House, 2001).

CHAPTER ELEVEN: SOCIAL MOBILIZATION CONFRONTS THE GREAT DEPRESSION

Before the rise of market economies, nature posed the single greatest unknown variable to food supply. A few years of bad grain harvests like those in France by 1789 could spur unrest and produce sustained calls for relief or change. By the time of France's second Revolution in 1848, and its subsequent reforms and remedies, climate did not disappoint the man in the street; the administration did.

While average mid-nineteenth century Frenchmen still made at least part of their living tilling the land, an increasing number based their lives in cities, and their livelihoods in crafts like milling, baking, or constructing wagons for the expanding commerce. In turn, their subsistence relied on the market of demand and supply. A rise in interest rates—on the funds borrowed to open a business—or an increase in taxes to fund a war, might prevent bakeries from paying their rent, forcing them to close. The bakers lose their livelihood, neighbors lose a food source, and money, not weather, becomes the culprit. In the case of 1848 France, the suspension of ameliorative policies, like subsidized training for rural men to learn urban skills, spurred marches on the financial and governmental districts in protest. That revolution and the ones that shortly followed across Europe—sometimes collectively called "Workers' Spring"—have much to tell us.

The course of political understanding of profound social and economic changes accompanying the industrial revolution has not been steady, especially regarding the ascendancy of movable wealth. Nothing better illustrates the point than the Great Depression. A bewildering stock market crash, the

retreat of investment in productive capacity, and the failure of most democratic societies to protect the security of their markets produced something
like an 1848 moment. The human consequences proved to be as severe as a
run of poor harvests or other widespread natural disaster.

> The stock market crash of 1929 had a cascade effect across institu-
> tions and people for the next three years. Historian Jill Lapore high-
> lights the scope of the those changes this way: American farmers were
> able to sell [only] about 10 percent of their crops. Creditors seized
> farms and sold them at auction...one in five banks failed... unemploy-
> ment rose [steadily] to 32 percent by 1932...by which time12 million
> Americans—a number equal to the entire population of the state of
> New York were out of work...In many homes family income fell to zero.
> One in four Americans suffered from want of food.[143]

The nineteenth century had seen panics in 1857 and 1873. What were
they about, and what made 1929 different?

The economic crisis of 1857, considered the first in an international
system just becoming aware of itself, was spawned, in the U.S. at least, by
two elements: the recently expanded stock market for railroad companies,
and the precious metals requirement for banks. Railroad stocks swelled in
value as more people moved west, especially into Kansas. When a major
trading company in Chicago—both a heavy user of railroad services and
significant holder of railroad and mortgage securities—failed, the bubble
burst. The subsequent sell-off led to a panic in shares of all kinds, especially
railroads and banks.

The second factor in the 1857 meltdown, which didn't run its course
until the Civil War, got underway in 1861 and involved the legal requirement
of the federal government for banks to hold a certain proportion of their
assets in gold and silver. In those days, trust in a trading partner demanded
a universally recognized valuable asset such as scarce metals. Seemingly just
a step up from barter, the cumbersome exchange failed to keep pace with
commercial change. And as we've come to see, bank failures bear the telltale
sign of persistent systemic weakness.

Railroads and growth figured into the crisis of 1873 as well. Some thought
the post-War boom an over expansion of capacity, particularly because
the federal government made large grants of land in the West to railroad
companies. That had the conflicting result of encouraging the growth but

---

[143] Lapore, 426.

also of fueling more debt incurred both by investors and builders. The boom didn't last and prices fell, assets shrank in value, businesses closed, layoffs followed.

Big challenges remained through the economy of the 1920s. A greater sense of urgency greeted Franklin Delano Roosevelt upon his 1932 election. Over twelve million people, close to thirty percent of the work force, were out of work. Charitable relief had dwindled. Shanty towns sprang up around cities, some within the grassy acres of Central Park in NYC. And long lines— for bread, for jobs, for soup—remain among the most enduring visuals of 1932. Undoubtedly, these factors had a huge influence in determining FDR's and the Democratic Party's victory.

In addition to the human and social challenges, what would become the New Deal faced technical and institutional hurdles. How should the government address the failures of free markets to self-correct, as Adam Smith said they would? Herbert Hoover, the incumbent president in 1932, continued to believe in the Invisible Hand, and promised "prosperity is just around the corner."

Someone needed to rethink *how*, not simply *whether*, our national government could use capitalism to serve the country more reliably. Such an effort needed to first focus on the supply of money, for industry needed adequate liquidity to create or re-open jobs. And at the correlate of that supply issue lay the very heart of the system: financial markets. The circulation of wealth— as a function of industrial investment in the competitive world of privately owned companies—became a prominent question.

Expedients sprang from Roosevelt's New Deal team almost at once: stabilize the banks and require that they keep a larger share of assets in reserve than before; create a Securities Exchange Commission and safeguard the unwary investor against speculative growth; encourage Congress to pass legislation establishing federal guarantees for depositor security. They also needed to empower the national bank to track fluctuations in the money supply, and control the rates charged for bank loans and mortgages. One of the most notable changes eventually moved interest rates from the pockets of major players in the financial market to a state-sponsored entity.

But only gradually. The price of gold in world markets continued to have a significant role in national policy regarding wealth supply for two-thirds of the remainder of the twentieth century. Since then, the substitute for that ancient assurance of value for commercial exchange has migrated to major national currencies held by multiple nations in their own treasuries, reflecting the confidence reposed in the economic—and, some would add, political—strength of major trading nations, especially Britain and the United States. Gold has come and gone, but money supply remains an issue of enormous importance.

FDR's Treasury kept borrowing rates low to facilitate investment by and in the private sector, but also allowed the government to prevent several New Deal relief programs from becoming too inflationary.

We know that these long-term institutional changes did not themselves generate enough demand for goods and services through an expanded work force to put the props back under a broken economy of such magnitude. Expansion of the country's productive capacity would take a while longer. Historians seem now agreed that a return to pre–1929 levels of economic activity did not occur until the U.S. prepared to enter World War II. The sovereign need to go to war, and subsequent re-armament, became the impetus for greater productive capacity. Essentially, what happened between the 1932 election until 1940 comes down to a simple restoration of self-respect found in a return to work.

Not dissimilar to what Bismarck did for Germany in the late 1800s, the most enduring initiatives of the New Deal included not only a return to work but a promotion of worker participation in the dynamics of production, and the offer of fairer chances at livable incomes. The most visible initiatives and agencies put people to work again in publicly useful jobs. The Civilian Conservation Corps (CCC), the Public Works Administration (WPA), and the Works Progress Administration (WPA) together harnessed the energies of thousands upon thousands of workers, many of them at the time unemployed or unskilled. These agencies funded the jobs directly or through private sector companies equipped to take on immense projects. While the government did not design these jobs to be permanent, and phased them out by the 1940s, worker participation—beyond the jobs at hand—became a sustained part of the U.S. economy.

Specifically, FDR pitched Congress the idea for a national agency similar to one he started while governor of New York:

> propose to create [the CCC] to be used in complex work, not interfering with normal employment [i.e., no competition for skilled workers] and confining itself to forestry, the prevention of soil erosion, flood control, and similar projects. I call your attention to the fact that this type of work is of definite, practical value, not only through

the prevention of great present financial loss but also as a means of creating future national wealth.[144]

The CCC provided jobs for young men with few skills and, at any one time, enrolled as many as three-hundred thousand. Through the course of its nine years in operation, three million young men (eighteen to twenty-five) participated in the CCC, which provided them with barracks style housing, clothing and food, together with a wage of $30 (about $570 in 2017) per month, twenty-five dollars of which they had to send home to their families. The men worked on natural lands areas under the control of federal or state government, increasing the visibility of those areas, and calling attention to the positive health effects of being out of doors. Moreover the work improved public accessibility to such scenic places as the Smokey Mountain National Park straddling the border between North Carolina and Tennessee.

The Public Works Administration (PWA), one of the core of measures adopted during FDR's famous First Hundred Days in the National Industrial Recovery Act (1933), sought to both stimulate the economy through major investments in infrastructure, and create viable jobs through private sector companies. Particular projects remain so visible and prominent that just listing them in one place gives a hint of the scale of the PWA. In New York City alone, these stand out: the Lincoln Tunnel, Triborough Bridge and LaGuardia Airport. The Hoover Dam gave work to ten thousand employees at one time. And the San Francisco Bay Bridge reflected a huge investment in regional infrastructure for generations. Key West's Ocean Bridge provided the first and only roadway to that storied community off the southern tip of Florida to and from the region's largest city, Miami.

In the spring of 1935 the Emergency Relief Appropriation Act became law and accomplished several things. It added more federal funds to the CCC and the PWA, extending their life and scope. Equally significant, the act created a kind of sister agency for infrastructure and unemployment relief. After two years of experience with the PWA oriented to the private sector, the Roosevelt administration realized it had not reached great pockets of the older, unskilled unemployed who did not qualify for CCC work because of their age. Consequently, they established the WPA—first called the Works *Progress* Administration, then from 1939 the Works *Projects* Administration. It employed more than three million people in its first year, and over its eight years that number rose to eight and a half million. The cost was on the order

---

[144] Samuel Rosenman, ed., *The Public Papers and Addresses of Franklin D. Roosevelt*, (New York: Random House, 1938-1950), 80-1.

of eleven million dollars. The organization built lots of highways and local public buildings plus more than a thousand city parks.

Two features of the WPA made it subject to criticism from multiple quarters. Labor found the agency stingy, with pay rates below those in the private sector, like the PWA projects that contracted with private companies. The WPA, on the other hand, used agency workers—a practice designed to appease private business and avoid competition with it. These "second class" workers typically had fewer skills and less experience. Moreover local politicians complained of bias among local Democratic appointees, pointing out that in the sister agency of PWA the choice of recipients was made in Washington.

But for the skill and experience of WPA's director it could have fared worse. Harry Hopkins, a social worker by training, was not only a leading ideas man for the President but he also had demonstrable skill in bringing factions together for common good. He also had the encouragement of First Lady Eleanor Roosevelt, which allowed him to lead the agency into unpredictable sectors. Hopkins launched projects that gave work to artists, musicians, actors and writers. The Federal Art Project, illustratively, employed artists to teach crafts in rural schools. The Music Project organized musicians to give local concerts and archive an aural version of the country's musical history. And the Theater Project brought plays to countless small towns, reaching an estimated audience of thirty million.

One particularly appealing example, the Federal Writers Project, established guide books for every state, major cities and connecting highways. Published for a public eager to learn more about their country, both historically and in the straitened circumstances of the Depression. David Kennedy, in *Freedom from Fear*, reports that the Guide Book series, according to critic Alfred Kazin, offered an "extraordinary contemporary epic and a New Deal foundation in the American inheritance."[145] Much of the artistic commentary sponsored or induced by the federal project openly criticized the America it revealed, even through widely displayed photographic essays. Kazin also noted a kind of "persistent patriotic nationalism," or the power to love what we know.[146] "It was as if the American people were poised to execute more social, political and economic innovation than ever before in their history

---

[145] Alfred Kazin, in *Freedom From Fear, the American People in Depression and War, 1929-1945*, by David Kennedy, (New York: Oxford University Press, 1999), 257.
[146] Kazin, in Kennedy, 257.

and in that moment felt the need to take a long look before moving on into the future that President Roosevelt was promising."[147]

Another consequence of the Emergency Relief Appropriations Act of 1935, The Rural Electrification Administration (REA) brought cheap power to the countryside of America by sponsoring the formation of non-profit electric cooperatives. The REA backed loans ensured the construction of generator plants and the erection of power lines and poles in otherwise open spaces. Fewer than two farms out of ten had electricity when REA began; ten years later, nine out of ten had it.

Not only did the newly available electricity bring running water to the kitchen sinks of our farms, it also brought electric lights and the radio to the living rooms of countless families. Notwithstanding Dwight D. Eisenhower's countrywide interstate highway system, established in the 1950s, electricity offered a link between town and country the likes of which we would not see again until the digital age.

Widespread employment in a recovering market economy necessitated structural support for the burgeoning workforce. The National Labor Relations Act—NLRA, the Wagner Act of 1935—gave statutory permanence to rights of collective bargaining through unions. As expected, membership in trade unions increased in a way no era since has matched. Equally important, the act established a permanent agency, the National Labor Relations Board, to oversee factory wide elections, union representation, and, with the use of the federal courts, enforce the provisions of the Wagner Act.

The Fair Labor Standards Act of 1938 further supported American workers by setting a forty-four-hour maximum work week, and a twenty-five cents per-hour minimum wage for most categories of employment. Those exempted were considerable in number, larger possibly in the aggregate than number of people working in factories and shops combined. Agricultural workers, people who tilled the soil, and those in domestic service were exempted from the Fair Labor Standards Act. The racial overtone to that exemption cannot be minimized given that much of the Congressional resistance to coverage was from southern Democrats of the 1930s, nominally members of the President's own party. The Act further forbade labor by anyone under the age of sixteen, and hazardous employment for anyone under the age of eighteen. However, 300,000 people profited from increased wages, and 1.3 million enjoyed reduced hours.

---

[147] Kazin, in Kennedy, 257.

Such a robust commitment to the American worker called for the institution of a new administrative post. Frances Perkins (1880–1965), the first
Secretary of Labor—and first woman cabinet member—proved herself to
FDR as a member of his gubernatorial administration, and brought with
her a well-developed sense of civic responsibility. As a social worker, she
had volunteered in one Jane Addams's settlement houses in Chicago. Later,
motivated by the New York City Triangle Shirt Waist Fire of 1911 in which
one hundred forty seamstresses died, Perkins pushed for state legislation
to protect against unsafe conditions. Like her colleague Harry Hopkins,
Frances Perkins gave her unwavering support to FDR and his New Deal.

Before she became Secretary of Labor, Perkins drafted what would
become the single most important, and certainly most symbolic program of
the New Deal: the Social Security Act. While its benefits would not mate-
rialize for some years, it established a permanent system of universal retirement pensions, unemployment insurance, and cash benefits for the handi-
capped and for fatherless children. By concentrating on many of our most
vulnerable citizens, it established a framework for the entire welfare system
of the country.

Significantly, Roosevelt wanted to finance social security not by under-
writing it with general federal revenues, thereby subjecting it to the vagaries
of budget cycles and partisan log rolling, but through payroll taxes. Drawing
benefits, upon retirement or other critical need, represented a form of earned
pension or guarantee against a temporary loss of a job for which the citizens
paid in advance. The act offered a simple promise in the wake of the Depression: those who work and pay taxes will be protected in their old age.

What would Rousseau think of the New Deal?

One. Rousseau would applaud the clear recognition of basic human
compassion as a driving force in the imagination of principal advisors
Frances Perkins and Harry Hopkins. Their ideas found their way into a
variety of New Deal initiatives. Both had brought their on-the-ground experience to the challenges of governing in a crisis, not unlike Rousseau who
had informed his writings with the experience of varied employments and
uncertain independence.

Two. He would support a focus on communitywide work enhancement
like the CCC and the PWA. His particular notice of such tasks in his native
Geneva is indicative. The "sovereignty" of all members of his version of the

social contract implies not mere formal civic duties like deliberating and voting, but also a direct role in the "doing" of the people's public work.

Three. The New Deal's National Labor Relations Act might strike Rousseau as a brilliant example of confronting one of his constant fears, that institutions—in this case a voluntary work relationship—invariably led to dominance by some over the many. At least with collective bargaining Rousseau could recognize that the state might be a reliable referee of fairness in the face of a very unequal balance of power.

Four. He might find the same kind of pleasant surprise reflected in the regulation of financial markets set up with the Securities Exchange Commission in the New Deal of the 1930s, because it represented investors in a faceless stock exchange against the raw power of capital managers to cheat or be careless in how the market actually behaved. Another example, arguably, that Rousseau mistrusted society's capacity for keeping institutions in humane check against a predictable growth of inequality.

Speculative though they are, the possible identifications made here about Rousseau and recent political and cultural developments long past his time might at least serve to focus on how any of us understand the interaction between thought and action, large or small. And when both thought and action are dynamic and continually changing, as in political philosophy and the history of politics, the impulse to summarize is large and hard to resist.

Chapter Twelve: Post World War Two Cooperation and Innovation

In the 1930s, the national government of United States moved decisively to come to grips with both the material scarcity brought on by the depression and the psychological blow to the country's vision and collective nerve. FDR avoided Herbert Hoover's jaded mantra of "rugged individualism" and rather, in his inaugural address, identified our common dilemma—how to overcome the veritable paralysis of the moment in the shared life of the nation. Famously declaring that the "only thing we have to fear is fear itself," he implicitly gave his fellow citizens a clap on the back and encouraged them to confront the enormity of it all with imagination and courage. And so we did.

The surge of initiative and response constituted nothing less than a social mobilization of America. Beyond visionary leadership with the strong determination of a president seemingly made for the times, the wrenching circumstances of the crash and Depression provided unique opportunity for genius, but, in equal measure, grit. By the time of his third four-year term as president—a first for the country—Roosevelt had to re-calibrate and determine what the 1940s would be about. While the effects of the Depression lingered, the president brooded over the dark clouds of war already forming in Europe and Asia.

Though the United States remained officially neutral until the Japanese attack on Pearl Harbor, as early as the summer of 1940 Roosevelt agreed with the British to swap fifty moth-balled destroyers for long term leases on a chain of airfields situated from Newfoundland to Trinidad. By early fall,

Congress instated the first peacetime draft, requiring men between the ages of twenty-one and thirty-six to register for military service. Roosevelt tried to prepare the country for what lay ahead, and in his first big rhetorical step, his address to Congress in January 1941, he introduced the Four Freedoms: Freedom of Faith, Freedom of Speech, Freedom from Want, and Freedom from Fear. The latter two themes had resonated throughout his earlier terms of office, and now, the other two—from our Bill of Rights—shifted into the center of Roosevelt's vision for the remainder of his time in office.

Polls showed that most Americans wanted to stay out of the war, but FDR continued the lay the groundwork for formal U.S. participation. By March 1941, still neutral, the U.S. agreed to provide direct military assistance to the countries already at war with Germany, Russia and Britain, by means of the Lend-Lease Act. In August 1941, after Britain had weathered the fury of the Blitz, Prime Minister Winston Churchill, anxious for his country's depth of resources and holding onto the prospect of America's active alliance, invited Roosevelt to the Atlantic Conference in Newfoundland. Together they issued a simple declaration, the Atlantic Charter, mostly for diplomatic and public relations purposes.

Once the Japanese attacked Pearl Harbor, triggering a Declaration of War from Congress on December 8, 1941, the country marshaled its resources in ways and on a scale never seen before. Factories went back into operation for the production of everything from trucks, tanks, and howitzers, to ships, planes, and ammunition. Back to work, back to little or no unemployment, and back to conscripted deployment. Over ten million men would serve during the course of World War II, leaving gaps in any number of roles stateside.

The armed forces instituted a variety initiatives including the Women's Army Corps (WAC) and the Women's Air Service Pilots (WASP) as well as the Ferry Command. And while women had long worked in the mills of the textile industry, they had not been "needed" in the more physical industrial sites like machine shops, shipyards, and aircraft factories. Selected Service, i.e., the draft, although applying only to able-bodied males, in effect precluded any gender restrictions for wartime employment, paving the way for Rosy-the-Riveter. Designed for this period and used vividly in advertisements for War Bonds and other voluntary civilian investments in the war effort, this iconic figure still stands for income equity between men and women in the twenty-first century.

In addition to providing greater employment opportunity than all the agencies combined, the war effected progress on yet another stateside front with measured racial inclusion. Sustained pressure from Philip Randolph, head of the Sleeping Car Porters Union, motivated FDR to issue Executive Order Number 8802, which prohibited discrimination based on race, creed, color, or national origin in defense industries. The armed forces, however, thanks largely to the continued dominance of old line Southern Democrats in Congress, remained separated. Although segregated by branch or unit, large numbers of African-Americans still got caught up in the vast net of the government's mobilization to fight. Some of those units achieved recognizable fame, including the Tuskegee Squadron of the Army Air Corps, who demonstrated what well educated and highly motivated young Black men could do, even if their country asked them to do it in isolation.

Other elements of the war effort affected the balance of daily life. Income taxes went up, and new taxes were launched. The Excess Profits Tax, intuitively fair in its conception, recognized that the urgency of public need outweighed ordinary procurement in the open market. Put another way, the tax acknowledged the government responsibility to ensure that private owners of production did not obtain an inflated price for their services while assisting the nation in one of its central purposes. From a capitalist's perspective, it offered a gentler policy than a government seizure of factories to operate them as state-managed industries.

A combination of initiatives, whether intentionally or not, built a kind of national camaraderie, often referred to as the "home front," to support the war effort. Rationing of scarce staples helped support a surging army and navy around the globe and included everything from sugar, butter, and meat, to gasoline and rubber, to iron, steel and aluminum. The rise in the value of basic metal spawned a new market in the private sector—scrap metal—that continued to flourish even after the war ended. As the war stretched on, it became clear that deprivation would continue to intensify as some goods became unavailable "for the duration" of the war. Silk, for example, used in army parachutes, disappeared from the market place, impacting fabrics like those used in women's stockings. The scarcity led to the DuPont Company's invention of workable synthetic substitutes —Rayon, then Nylon—that quickly became restricted as well, feeding an already robust black market.

Along with industrial innovation, the war effort spawned revolutionary advances in advertising and public relations. Design creativity, around a narrowed ambit of ideas and products we might call propaganda if used by our adversaries, promoted slogans like "Loose Lips Sink Ships" or songs like "Let's Remember Pearl Harbor... as we did the Alamo!" An elementary form of censorship also came into play, though it usually did not go much beyond redacting letters to or from active duty armed services members.

Hollywood did its part to bolster morale and encourage broad political support for the war efforts, as well. Studios delivered appealing stories about life in embattled allied countries, like *Mrs. Miniver*, set in Blitz-devastated London, starring Deborah Kerr and Walter Pidgeon. Beginning in 1942, in the early months of the war, the industry delivered a steady supply of movies about American forces in action. Films like *Guadalcanal Diary*, starring John Wayne, depicted hard-fought campaigns like that in the Pacific Ocean's Solomon Island chain.

War time mobilization produced a mixed bag of changes. Both liberty and equality would take some hits of varied duration and impact. The most notorious example from civilian life in America's World War II experience affecting both those ideals came packaged in President Roosevelt's 1942 Executive Order 9066. It authorized military officials on the West Coast to declare certain areas—army posts or shipyards, for example—restricted, and from which persons of Japanese ancestry could be excluded. The 1982 Congressional Commission on Wartime Relocation and Internment of Civilians, *Personal Justice Denied*, found that in violation of orders issued under this authority "some 120,000 people were held without judicial review." The report further concluded that "not a single documented act of espionage, sabotage, or fifth column activity was committed by an American citizen of Japanese ancestry or by a resident Japanese alien on the West Coast."[148]

Contemporary initiatives to confront the orders and their individual impacts were made through the courts.[149] The legacy of the decisions from the Supreme Court in 1943 and 1944 are themselves artifacts of the era for the light they shine on continuing issues of national security versus personal liberty.[150]

David Kennedy reflects on the implications of wider scope especially relevant to themes of this book:

> What happened to the Japanese was especially disquieting in wartime America precisely because it so loudly mocked the nation's best image of itself as a tolerantly inclusive, fair-minded, "melting pot" society— an image long nurtured in national mythology, and one

---

[148] Congressional Commission on Wartime Relocation and Internment of Civilians, *Personal Justice Denied*, (Washington, D.C., 1982), 3.

[149] See Eugene Rostow, "The Japanese American Cases—A Disaster," *Yale Law Journal*, 54 no. 3, (June 1945), 489.

[150] Stephen Dycus, Arthur L. Berney, William C. Banks, and Peter Raven-Hansen, *National Security Law*, (Philadelphia: Walters Kluwer, 2007) 703-714.

powerfully reinforced by the conspicuously racialized conflict that was World War II.[151]

Meanwhile, in the penultimate year of the War, Congress enacted the Servicemen's Readjustment Act, more popularly known as the GI Bill of Rights, in April 1944. The program provided college tuition to anyone who had served in the armed services during the war, many of whom might not have otherwise have even finished high school when they re-entered civilian life in the mid-to late 1940s. Other benefits included low-interest home mortgages and small business loans, as well as unemployment payments for one year. Congress renewed the act several times before the 2017 adoption of the Forever GI Bill.

The collective benefit of helping educate and otherwise provide assistance to young adults enhances the economy's productive capacities and, hopefully, inspires a larger measure of civic engagement in our local communities. The link to service in wartime distinguishes assistance to veterans from other federal expenditures, and the post-World War II experience stands in stark contrast to the failed initiatives to do something comparable in the wake of previous wars. We do not think of such benefits as welfare, yet we can see an unmistakable equivalence, both in terms of individual advancement as well as in terms of social cohesion and stability. Not since the creation in Lincoln's administration of the Land Grant Colleges program—the Morrill Act of 1862—had the government invested so extensively in higher education.

By the spring of 1945, President Roosevelt had done all he would for the nation. Upon his death, Harry S. Truman picked up the reins and went on to finish much of the progressive, inclusive work FDR started.

Perhaps challenged by the example of another Democratic president— Woodrow Wilson's failure to convince the U.S. legislators to join the League of Nations—Roosevelt still hoped that something good, even idealistic, could grow out of the carnage of war. Not long after he died, diplomatic and political advisors like Edward R. Stettinius launched an international conference in San Francisco, the design for what would become the United Nations. This time the U.S. Senate agreed to adopt the post-war treaty, and thus the United States became a founding member of the international peacekeeping organization.

One of the first and most visible of its programs, the UN Relief and Rehabilitation Agency (UNRRA), distributed about $4 billion worth of

---

[151] Dycus et al., *National Security Law*, 760.

food, medicine, tools, and farm implements in the four years it operated. The agency served nations especially hard hit by starvation, dislocation, and political chaos. Many of UNRAA's functions gradually transferred to permanent UN agencies, including the International Refugee Organization and the World Health Organization, which continue that spirit of cooperation today.

Historically, the bold, newfound international cooperation marked the first time that a large number of independent nation states collaboratively recognized the scope of social and humanitarian needs and came to together to confront their challenges. Through cooperation and the pooling of resources and skills, even disparate sovereignties formed something larger than any one of them could mount for itself—a combination Rousseau could not have imagined. Some of his followers, like Marquis de Condorcet (1743–1794), might have, though. Condorcet went so far as to imagine an equality that included not only both women and men but all races and nations.

Just as the broad vision of the Universal Declaration of the Rights of Man and Citizen in 1789 must have inspired Condorcet, it could well have inspired the UN founders a century and a half later. At the end of World War II, universal appreciation for human need motivated fifty-one countries to, among other things, "reaffirm faith in fundamental human rights, in the dignity and worth of the human person, in the equal rights of men and women and of nations large and small."[152] Their effort also succeeded because the United States, the nation with the lion's share of material resources still intact, had ready and willing leadership for it.

The war ended, the United Nations emerged, and Britain, like the United States, embraced a change in leadership. In 1945, the Labour Party succeeded in seizing the nation's mandate from the Conservatives, replacing the wartime coalition led by Winston Churchill. Labour's leader, Clement Atlee (1883–1967), had none of Churchill's stump appeal, but what he lacked in charisma, he more than made up for with ideas and ability to judge the nation's mood. In 1906, two years out of Oxford, he became a volunteer at Haileybury House, a charitable club for working-class boys in the East End of London, run by his old school. From 1907 to 1909 he served as the club's manager, during which time the poverty and deprivation he encountered challenged his conservative political views. Eventually, they gave way to the understanding that private charity would never sufficiently alleviate poverty, and that only state-directed action and income redistribution would have

---

[152] Preamble to the U.N. Charter, in Mary Ann Glendon, *A World Made New, Eleanor Roosevelt and the Universal Declaration of Human Rights*, (New York: Random House, 2002), 18.

any serious effect. He converted to socialism, joined the Independent Labour Party (ILP), and became active in local politics.

Reflecting nothing short of a seismic shift in the consciousness of the British people, Labour's victory extinguished a century's worth of power arrangements favoring the traditions of land, finance and industry and the established leadership class made up of Etonians and Ox-bridge alumni. The political reforms of the nineteenth century finally paid off, as the levers of government moved into the hands of miners, factory workers, state school graduates, and trade unionists. Certainly J.S. Mill would have approved, while Herbert Spencer most likely would not have.

Before the remarkable shift of Britain's politics, reformers managed to advance basic socialist ideas in the wake of World War I, most notably in the development of public housing for returning war veterans. Government control of the railroads, instituted during World War II, shifted to full blown nationalization with the Transport Act of 1947. And a year later, in 1948, the sentiment that everyone needs and is responsible for health maintenance, gave rise to the National Health Service (NHS), an idea that seems as compatible with capitalism as limits on hours and ages of employment.

The two men who founded the NHS represented the new kind of political leadership emerging in Britain. Aneurin Bevan (1897-1960) came from a Welsh coal mining family, and though incompletely educated, he worked in the mines and earned his leadership skills in the trade union movement. William Beverage (1879-1963), son of a British member of the Indian Civil Service, studied his country's social policy as an economist at Oxford. He became a key player in the early days of progressive politics when David Lloyd George led the Liberal Party from 1906 to 1914, during which time a form of health insurance emerged that was jointly supported by contributions from employees and employers. After advising the administration on manpower issues during the Great War, he became Director of the London School of Economics. Tasked in 1941 with drawing up a plan for rebuilding Britain after World War II, he published a report in 1942, "Social Insurance and Allied Services Cmd. 6404," addressing the "five giants on the road to reconstruction" of "Want... Disease, Ignorance, Squalor and Idleness." The report lay dormant until Labour's Attlee breathed life into it for his new government after World War II. The Beverage Report ultimately functioned as a blueprint for the welfare state, widely read in the capitals of the industrialized Western nations.

There's little doubt that the Liberal Party's time under David Lloyd George fed the pool of experience that led to Labor's ascendency following the next war. The influence of crisis—and its companions, scarcity and sacrifice—produced the conditions and a new mind-set for the dramatic changes the Labor Party brought to flower under Clement Attlee. The sheer grit displayed by every class of citizen, urban or rural, worker or shop-keeper, and shared sense of participation of volunteers and conscripts in the armed forces touched even well-to-do families. Moreover, the wealthy, too, had to contend with material shortages of everyday consumer goods and the attendant rationing restrictions. The war tempered the disparities of class still underlying British life, as everyone pitched in to do their bit. And Churchill cultivated that spirit throughout the war.

By the end of the war, the sacrifice and hard work had spawned a clear consciousness of something very powerful in the midst of Britons over the whole of the country. United and undefeated, their common efforts had saved the country from invasion and complete devastation. The sharing of common purpose coupled with an awareness of common effort produced a moment, it seems, ripe for change. They needed only to find leadership equal in imagination to the promise of that moment. The Labour Party's time had come.

Any plans would have to acknowledge the stark reality of the country—from ravaged factories, dockyards, and homes to severally disrupted agriculture and trade. Rationing lasted into the 1950s. The country, especially the larger cities, needed restoring, if not rebuilding— bridge by bridge, store by store, school by school. Cities presented the bigger challenge, especially London, hit so hard by the Blitz of 1940.

Though it's satisfying to dwell on the shared work and sacrifice that produced a solidarity across the demographics and strata of British society, such an impression distorts somewhat the reality of that time. Angus Calder, in *The People's War, Britain 1939–45*, has gone beyond that customary version of the times to claim that the civilian war effort raised consciousness among ordinary people, especially among urban marginals, engendering a demand for more respect.[153]

The labor movement, with help from people like Aneurin Bevan, organized more aggressively and watched their party move to the front of the new national energy bursting from the throes of war into the prosaic business of peace renewed. The change in the nation's political consciousness witnessed a parallel development in Britain's colonial territories. A new form of non-violent protest at the hands of Mohandas Gandhi (1869–1948)—passive

---

[153] Angus Calder, *The People's War, 1939-45*, (New York: Pantheon Books, 1969), 17.

resistance to Britain's long imperial rule of India—added another dynamic to the independence movements already in play. Gandhi trained as a lawyer in the UK; he first put his skills to use in South Africa. Accustomed to protest, he readily conceded that his non-violent strategy would not have worked against a totalitarian regime because passive resistance, it seems, only works if the overlords possess the capacity for being shamed into doing the right thing. The lessons of the movement were not wasted on other civil rights leaders since then, notably Dr. Martin Luther King Jr, in the United States.

Labor Party members did not expect or promote indigenous movements like Quit India, but their manifesto had long distrusted imperialism and its role in maintaining the dominance of private commerce and banking that lay at the center of nineteenth century capitalism. And though their concern remained primarily with reform at home and less with the independence of colonial people overseas, in the end, both gained in Labor's post-war ascendancy.

Broader implications accompanied the sea-change in Britain's domestic political consciousness. The two wartime leaders wielding the most power among the Allies, Roosevelt and Churchill, differed over whether and how to declare a set of goals for fighting Germany and, later, Japan. At their Atlantic Conference shipboard meeting in 1940, both leaders recognized the need for a public relations statement in the U.S. to increase civilian support for the country's possible entry into the war. Roosevelt wanted to foresee the independence of colonial territories around the world, including both for those they would fight—like Japan, which controlled Korea and Manchuria—as well as those who were allies, like France, Britain, and the Netherlands. Against his own preferences as an imperialist and traditional conservative, Churchill agreed to the bargain, even if, at the time, he could not have foreseen Atlee and Labour's rise to power in 1945. It was not, after all, a Tory government that had to confront the shrinking of the Empire.

CHAPTER THIRTEEN: COLD WAR DIVISIONS DRIVE DEBATE AND CHANGE

The world sighed in relief when the most destructive war in recorded history ended. Optimism about the future of civilization, born of that moment, reigned. Then Winston Churchill delivered his Iron Curtain speech, from Westminster College in Missouri in 1946, and fundamentally divergent views on governance took hold on opposing sides of that curtain. Two more years would pass before the Berlin Airlift demonstrated the new reality of the Cold War. The broader consensus defined by the United Nations and its agencies included only Western democracies and not the eastern bloc dominated by the Soviet Union, who effectively recused itself from international cooperation.

Joint efforts to deal with millions of displaced persons and the other major calamities of the war gave way to suspicion, antipathy, and ideological sniping. The new kind of warfare included efforts to undermine the other camp—Communist versus Capitalist—in the eyes of the remaining uncommitted or non-aligned nations. Large countries like Indonesia and India as well as smaller ones like many of the states of Africa self-identified as the "third world." Along the continental fringes of Europe and Southeast Asia, the surrogates of the blocs—like Greece and Malaysia, formerly British Malaya—fell into combat euphemized as civil war. Viet Nam offered a more complicated story, filled with unwavering Communist rule despite expensive and destructive American intervention.

By the late 1950s and early 1960s, the Soviet Union and the United States, as leaders of their respective blocs, moved beyond merely treating one another as military threats but as objects of propaganda in the form of derision. In 1958, Nikita Khrushchev, Premier of the Soviet Union, famously told then-Vice President Richard Nixon that communism would "bury" capitalism. Two years later, John F. Kennedy accused Nixon, his Republican opponent, of failing to meet the challenge of Russia's larger arsenal of long range missiles, making an alleged "missile gap" a key part of his presidential campaign.

Diplomatic efforts to confront the overhanging threat of "mutually assured destruction" successfully established a tenuous cooperation, resulting in test ban treaties and arms limitation agreements. However, the treaties more or less insured that the ideological war would continue unabated. The Soviets had Pravda and Izvestia as the official news sources of its claims about and denunciations of Western intentions and practices wherever they could identify them.

The rampant paranoia regarding communist subversion of our own institutions illustrates one of the Soviets' greatest achievements. Senator Joseph McCarthy's public attack on the State Department and the Army gave history the term McCarthyism, which carried such stigma that the real truth seldom made a difference. Many actors and others associated with the film industry, suspected of ties to the Communist Party, its doctrine or propaganda, found themselves blacklisted, defamation of the sort from which few recovered.

Russians particularly liked to besmirch America and its institutions for the increasingly obvious fact of Afro-American second-class citizenship.

When Dr. Martin Luther King, Jr. began his campaigns for racial justice in the South, Izvestia carried each of the marches in detail, giving prominence to the clashes between the police and protesters in various cities. Though FBI Director J. Edgar Hoover opened a file on King and had his phone tapped for years, King had no Soviet ties. In fact, some Soviet propaganda portrayed him as an Uncle Tom on the government payroll.

With the exception of the formation of the NAACP in 1909, we did not see a sustained national effort to confront the reality of racial subjection in the wake of Reconstruction. By the 1950s, however, a steady stream of leaders emerged from the Afro-American churches—always centers of community life—to challenge the status quo.

A year after the *Brown v. the Board of Education* decision that declared "separate but equal" schools a violation of the Fourteenth Amendment's Equal Protection clause, little had changed. State legislatures had yet to address discrimination in public facilities and services beyond schools. Rosa

Parks and Dr. King's followers moved things along with the 1955 bus boycott in Montgomery, Alabama. It took over a year, multiple lawsuits and injunctions, and a Supreme Court decision, but eventually the Black community prevailed and buses became integrated. Thus the civil rights campaigns and clashes of the 1960s began with those most directly affected by the Jim Crow regime.

The Greensboro and Nashville lunch counter sits-ins followed in 1960 and also became symbols of the movement. Despite their pacific intentions, the protestors often met with physical violence. Again, the protestors' resolve and leaders like John Lewis saw them through, and by late July, Greensboro had desegregated its lunch counters. In Nashville, the sit-ins extended to retail boycotts, forcing the majority of shops, restaurants, and even movie theatres to integrate by summer's end.

Dr. Martin Luther King Jr.'s 1963 "I Have a Dream" speech marks the spirit and visibility of the movement for civil rights. Close to half a million people—a record at the time—poured into the capital and gathered at the Lincoln Memorial for The Poor Peoples' March on Washington. Despite the violence associated with the boycotts, marches, and sit-ins, this huge gathering remained orderly. At day's end the same half million people quietly dispersed and returned to their homes, many far from that city, with the words King delivered to the attentive crowd surrounding the Reflecting Pools echoing in their hearts:

> There are those who are asking the devotees of civil rights, "When will you be satisfied?" We can never be satisfied as long as the Negro is the victim of the unspeakable horrors of police brutality. We can never be satisfied as long as our bodies, heavy with the fatigue of travel, cannot gain lodging in the motels of the highways and the hotels of the cities. We cannot be satisfied as long as the Negro's basic mobility is from a smaller ghetto to a larger one. We can never be satisfied as long as our children are stripped of their selfhood and robbed of their dignity by signs stating "for whites only." We cannot be satisfied as long as a Negro in Mississippi cannot vote and a Negro in New York believes he has nothing for which to vote. No, no, we are not satisfied and we will not be satisfied until justice rolls down like waters and righteousness like a mighty stream.[154]

A year later, King received international recognition for his place in America's unsteady search for racial justice. His Nobel Peace Prize Speech,

---

[154] Lapore, *These Truths*, 609-10.

delivered in Oslo in December of 1964, displays both a personal humility and a strength of mind that gave King's words the gravitas his movement had earned, even as its goals still seemed elusive:

> I conclude that this award which I receive on behalf of that move-ment is a profound recognition that nonviolence is the answer to the crucial political and moral question of our time—the need for man to overcome oppression and violence without resorting to violence and oppression. Civilization and violence are antithetical concepts. Negroes of the United States, following the people of India, have demonstrated that nonviolence is not sterile passivity, but a powerful moral force which makes for social transformation. Sooner or later all the people of the world will have to discover a way to live together in peace, and thereby transform this pending cosmic elegy into a creative psalm of brotherhood. If this is to be achieved, man must evolve for all human conflict a method which rejects revenge, aggression and retali-ation. The foundation of such a method is love.

> The tortuous road which has led from Montgomery, Alabama, to Oslo bears witness to this truth. This is a road over which millions of Negroes are traveling to find a new sense of dignity. This same road has opened for all Americans a new era of progress and hope. It has led to a new Civil Rights Bill, and it will, I am convinced, be widened and lengthened into a super highway of justice as Negro and white men in increasing numbers create alliances to overcome their common problems.

> I accept this award today with an abiding faith in America and an audacious faith in the future of mankind. I refuse to accept despair as the final response to the ambiguities of history...[155]

Nonviolence, King contended, is a "powerful moral force which makes for social transformation"[156] and lends dignity to those who live by its call to brotherhood. The eloquence of that moment would be tested, and for many betrayed, in the remaining years of the 1960s.

Ironically, 1964 was the same year that the U.S. war in Vietnam took a hard turn toward escalation with the Gulf of Tonkin Resolution in Congress. King's views on the war and those of LBJ inversely mirrored each other. King considered the war an expression of Western imperialism, lately revived under the guise of anti-communism. The condescension toward

---

[155] *The New York Times*, October 15, 1964, 1.
[156] *The New York Times*, October 15, 1964, 1.

colonial people around the world paralleled the treatment of Afro-American citizens in the U.S.—formally "free" but really held back from a broader, deeper equality with other Americans.

Although Martin Luther King Jr. is best known for his leadership of the campaign for racial equality at home, he was a persistent critic of U.S. policies abroad as well. In the decade after 1956, following his emergence as a national figure, King offered sporadic criticism of selected foreign policy issues within the general framework of Cold War anticommunism. He first opposed American involvement in Vietnam in 1965, but he abandoned his antiwar stance in the face of unexpectedly sharp attacks.

King's failed efforts in Chicago in 1966 led to a change in his critique of the Cold War. Previously, he had tended to separate domestic issues from foreign affairs, but now he saw the two as intertwined. Thomas Noer contends that King now viewed the Vietnam War through a more radical lens, one that equated U.S. involvement with neocolonialism, economic self-interest, and ingrained racism. King continued this more militant dissent until his assassination in April 1968.[157]

Johnson found the connection between civil rights at home and "freedom" for overseas populations inescapably tied to the ongoing competition with Communist influence around the world. He was not alone in that view. He and his advisors, like Secretary of State Dean Rusk and Secretary of Defense Robert McNamara, held the deep seated conviction of a sustained and comprehensive competition between two irreconcilable systems—only recently thrust on the world by the Iron Curtain and its commanding corollaries—like capitalism versus communism or freedom versus central planning. From that perspective, they considered any activity not affecting national loyalty of secondary concern.

Lyndon Baines Johnson, president from 1963 to 1968, came to the office in the wake of Kennedy's assassination in November of 1963. Not merely for that reason, but because Johnson used that office for so wide a range of domestic policy initiatives, he is identified here as the second major public figure of 1960s America. His speech at the University of Michigan in 1964 is said to be the formal launch of his core idea for the next four years. "The Great Society rests on abundance and liberty for all. It demands an end to

---

[157] Thomas J. Noer, "M.L. King and the Cold War," *Peace and Change* 22 no. 2 (April 1997), 111-131.

poverty and racial injustice, to which we are totally committed in our time. But that is just the beginning," Johnson declared.[158]

Before his term of office ended, Johnson could see that his domestic reforms were undercut by the country's war in Vietnam dividing young and old, the well-educated and the less educated—with a disproportionate number of the draftees being drawn from the latter group. The impact of that war on the social and cultural commonalities of previous generations, we see more clearly now, was severe.

Civil Rights

Historians like Randall Woods and Allan Brinkley of the LBJ era (1963–1969) agree that the most important success domestically was translating core demands of the civil rights movement into law (Woods 557; Brinkley 472). Four civil rights Acts were passed, including three in the first two years of Johnson's presidency. The Civil Rights Act of 1964 forbade job discrimination and outlawed segregation in public accommodations like hotels and restaurants. The Montgomery bus boycott finally paid off, nine years from its inception.

The Voting Rights Act of 1965 aimed to give new protections for minority voter registration and voting itself. It outlawed the use of literacy or other voter-qualification tests—such as reading passages of the text of the Constitution—that had served to keep African-Americans off voting lists during the long life of Jim Crow in the states of the former Confederacy. It also authorized federal lawsuits to end discriminatory poll taxes, whose justification never passed Supreme Court challenge. These taxes had affected many Afro-Americans as well as poverty-stricken White voters.

The 1965 Act also reinforced the Civil Rights Act of 1964 by authorizing the appointment of federal voting examiners in areas that, based on historic practices state by state, did not meet voter-participation requirements. This seems to have been unique as a kind of remedial innovation looking to check patterns of discrimination that could be expected to continue if there were no federal intervention.

The Civil Rights Act of 1968, reaching deeper into the private market system than its 1964 predecessor had done, banned housing discrimination, in both sales and rentals. It also extended constitutional protections to Native Americans on reservations.

---

[158] Lyndon B. Johnson, "Remarks at the University of Michigan, May 22, 1964," *Public Records of the Presidents*, 1963-1964, 704-7.

The Legal Service Corporation, a spin off from the Office of Economic Opportunity (OEO), brought the formal promise of "equal justice under law" to a greater measure of fulfillment on the civil side of justice. Whereas the right to counsel (from the Sixth Amendment) obtained in federal courts for criminal cases (and by extension through the 14th Amendment to the states since 1964), there was no general recognition of the legal needs of the poor in ordinary civil matters, whether involving litigation or not. Equality before the law, an explicit ideal as old as the French Revolution, was finally realized in this initiative. Such an ideal could scarcely be met without paying for it from public expenditures.

EEOC: Equal Employment Opportunity Commission

One of the most enduring of the Johnson era initiatives, this federal agency adjudicates disputes in the work place beyond the protections of the New Deal labor legislation—principally for the basics of collective bargaining plus working hours and conditions. The 1964 Civil Right Act provides for the agency's intervention and investigation into any employee's complaint of discrimination, whether based on race, sex, or religion. Age-related discrimination was added two years later. This new commission was empowered to investigate such complaints and issue orders when findings warranted, and, where appropriate, even evoked fines for violation of the employee's right to an environment free from the social harm of bias, including that instilled by the atmosphere of the place of employment. In other words, the employer is not free to ignore what co-workers do, any more than they can ignore what management or the corporation itself does.

The continued viability of this program bespeaks the progress made in erecting and maintaining work place conditions beyond anything early reformers had envisioned, say, in the time of the Progressives or Bismarck and his version of the welfare state. The advent of an EEOC also underscores the contemporary complexity of our society, both in terms of demographics and of sensibilities. A list of Discrimination by Type on the commissions website shows how extensive job-related protections have become since FDR's basic labor legislation thirty years earlier: sexual harassment or bias in hiring or compensation on account of race or color, religion, age, gender, and/or disability.

The combined effect of these initiatives has in recent times been likened to nothing short of a "second Reconstruction" by one involved observer, Dr. Rev. William J. Barber.[159]

Health Care: Senior Citizens and (Some) Others

The pressure felt in the nation's capital during the 1960s to extend civil rights for voting protections and new safeguards against discrimination even in the private sector did not extend to the other major realms of Johnson's Great Society. On the other hand, relevant ideas remained yet unfulfilled from earlier periods of reform. President Franklin Roosevelt had wanted to protect older citizens not only from the financial insecurity of retirement but also from the predictable decline of health in later years. As early as the 1880s in Germany, and Britain after World War II, health care assistance had become a feature of Europe's response to industrialization's human costs.

In 1930s America, however, FDR was cautious of pushing too fast in that direction lest he jeopardize other parts of his legislative agenda. Thus he did not include medical care assistance in the Social Security Act of 1935. Not long after he became president, following Roosevelt's death, Harry S. Truman pitched the idea to Congress in 1945 and again in 1949. Both times he faced an intense lobbying effort when the American Medical Association claimed that "socialized medicine" would interfere with the doctor–patient relationship. By the 1950s, the idea lay dormant through the eight Eisenhower years.

With John F. Kennedy's inauguration in 1961, the effort gained steam once again—especially among those who appreciated the New Deal. Kennedy made medical care part of his New Frontier and he campaigned on the issue. The major opposition then came from fiscal conservatives, including some congressional Democrats like Wilbur Mills of Arkansas. This time, health insurance companies joined the medical profession in lobbying against the move. In the interim, that industry had gained a significant stakeholder role in the debate: under amended IRS rules, companies paying their employees' premiums could earn a tax deduction. In the end, it was left to LBJ's presidency to overcome the opposition. In the 1964 election, Democrats not only won the White House but also majorities in the Congress, where, for time in decades, liberal Democrats outnumbered the coalition of Republicans and Southern Democrats.[160]

---

[159] William J. Barber, *The Third Reconstruction: How a Moral Movement is Overcoming the Politics of Division and Fear*, (Boston: Beacon Press, 2016), 118-19.

[160] Julian E. Zelizer, "How Medicare Was Made," *New Yorker Magazine*, Feb. 15, 2015. When the Social Security Act of 1965 was passed, Johnson traveled to Independence, Missouri,

A sister program under the 1965 Social Security Act for a broader portion of the public has had less success. Medicaid was designed to cover medical services for persons of all ages who lacked the means to purchase it in the private market or did not have it where they worked. Two design features in particular render it inadequate as a national program: one, a state must choose to run such a program and take a ten percent participatory role; two, the scope and eligibility requirements are set by the states individually.[161]

Education

Political and civil rights—as concepts, at least—have intertwined with theories of democratic governance since the revolutions of the eighteenth century. Nothing so explicit formed around health care and access to it in the theories or examples of self-governance for most of the nineteenth century. Calls to "promote the general welfare," found in such places as the Constitution of the United States, could be liberally construed as covering those human needs, too. Although long delayed, something like that interpretation found a widespread application in the twentieth century.

In contrast, the availability of general education has remained central to the creation of governments based on citizen participation. Every major thinker we have studied has emphasized the role of education for citizenship as well as for individual development. Rousseau, Jefferson, Robert Owen, J.S Mill—all of them made it a central concern.

In the case of a federal republic like that of the United States of America, the role of education—its support and administration—has been left to the responsibility of individual states. That, of course, was where all government in the America of the late eighteenth century resided, after independence but before the Confederation *or* the federal Constitution. The wording of state constitutions typically make that coverage explicit.

Two corollaries stem from that historic happenstance. One is that the realities of relative wealth and commitment among the states produced a pattern of diverse funding and effectiveness. In the second, the fact of state responsibility for education itself built a kind of mindset—one might say jealousy—in favor of the local control of schools. So much so that through most of the country's history it became conventional wisdom that we should leave the national government to play little or no role—at least at the level

and signed it into law with Harry Truman and his wife Bess proudly looking on.
[161] Continuing efforts to improve this model were made under the Clinton administration without success, then again under the Obama administration through the Affordable Care Act of 2010.

of primary and secondary education. That situation changed dramatically in the Johnson administration of the 1960s. The Elementary and Secondary Education Act of 1965 authorized a $1.1 billion program of grants to states for allocations to school districts with larger numbers of children of low-income families.

The act also established Head Start—originally started by the OEO as an eight-week summer program—continuing existence. It gave substance to the promise of an education of quality and equality made implicitly in the *Brown v. Board Education* decision from the Supreme Court in 1954. Children from homes with little or no support for reading and the other basic grade school skills would have a new hope for greater capacity for achievement once they were formally enrolled in those classes.

Colleges and universities received federal dollars, too, in the Johnson era, for both buildings such as libraries and for aid to students for tuition and fees. Eventually these tapered off into direct loan assistance to students, notably Pell grants which continue to this time.

One of the most enduring effects of federal aid to colleges appeared as a renewed effort to equalize institutional support for women's sports teams with that of men's. The now famous Title IX provision was added to Johnson era legislation in 1972 under Republican president Richard Nixon. This initiative exemplifies the interaction of civil rights oversight in federal legislation on one hand and, on the other, direct assistance to educational institutions across the full spectrum of academic disciplines and facilities. As with the Morrell Act's (Land Grant Colleges, 1862) support for higher education in the nineteenth century, the nation again was called to recognize the long term wisdom of investment in the advancement of personal development of all citizens. The bonds of community are strengthened by both promoting equal access—something courts enforced—and by enhancing the capacities of individuals—something federal legislation granted.

Anti-Poverty Programs

Of the many domestic initiatives launched under the Johnson administration, none was quite as ambitious as that called "the war on poverty." It was large by any precedent since the New Deal, but also progressive, or experimental, in the ideas undergirding it. The metaphor of a "war" for various federal initiatives, either actually started or only suggested, like the war on drugs or war on crime, perhaps met its rhetorical limits in a set of programs cutting across so much of civic life as one that was intended to address, in Johnson's own words 'hunger, illiteracy and unemployment' in 1960s America. The centerpiece of the War on Poverty was the Economic Opportunity Act of 1964, which created an Office of Economic Opportunity (OEO) to oversee a variety of community-based antipoverty programs.

Under that agency no fewer than six programs were started at that time: Head Start, for pre-school preparation in poorer neighborhoods; Job Corps, to assist in acquiring marketable skills by youth from poor families; Neighborhood Youth Corps, to provide actual work experience; VISTA (Volunteers in Service to America), a domestic version of the Peace Corps; Upward Bound, to assist the transition from high school to college by youth from lower income families; and Community Health Centers. Moreover, Johnson extended and made permanent the notable example of direct public assistance for families living below the poverty line known as Food Stamps, begun in the Kennedy administration.

A belief held by Johnson—a former high school teacher—as well as by principal advisors like Bill Moyers and Richard Goodwin, formed the foundation and motivating energy for these programs. Simply put, the idea was to create not a "top-down" or "ready-made" agency for a community, but to have members of that community design and administer it. The experience of the locale would count more than what outsiders might invent for it. This idea was embodied in the common thread of "community action." Cities or counties could apply for grants and guidance from the OEO for locally organized and directed projects touching the various agency goals. Practice in the arts of democracy was an unspoken goal of all these community action programs. A book being widely read at that time was *The Other America*, by Michael Harrington (1962), in which neighborhood building was just as much the aim as material improvements through jobs or job-training.

The Nixon and Ford administrations dismantled the Office of Economic Opportunity, largely by transferring poverty programs to other government departments. President Ronald Reagan's 1981 budget further cut funding for many of these programs.

As with those of the New Deal of the 1930s, some of the initiatives from the Great Society aspiration lasted longer than others. From the New Deal, social security and the labor reform acts, like Fair Labor Standards and the National Labor Relations Board prevail as fixtures of modern America's governing institutions. Likewise, the Civil Rights acts of the Johnson years have continued to guide our progress in confronting racial bias and more than one kind of discrimination. Medicare from the '60s similarly reflects the reality of the vulnerability of age that brought FDR's signature initiative to the front of our social concerns as a nation.

It would be an exaggeration to say that a strong consensus on confronting economic inequality in bold, new ways lasted much beyond the Johnson (Vietnam) era. Even so, the country mounted real initiatives that remain in the vocabulary of public discourse. The mere fact that the federal government launched an Office of Economic Opportunity goes well beyond mere reformist talk. What's more, we continue to mine the reports of its related programs like Head Start and Upward Bound as well as Teacher Corps to learn what we may from concentrated efforts to co-join opportunity with community engagement to set priorities and build supporting local networks of civic and professional leadership.[162]

In the wake of the renewed reach for greater equality in the United States, especially a more determined push for equality of opportunity in the 20th century, economist Richard Pomfret, in *The Age of Equality: The Twentieth Century in Economic Perspective*, offers this summary:

The limits of the welfare state would be debated in the 1980s. Did unemployment insurance, high tax rates, and other social security and redistribution measures dull incentives? Should benefits be universal, provided as a right, or should they be targeted to reach those most in need, even if the necessary means-testing imposes a stigma on recipients? To what extent should health, education, and pensions be privately funded, and how should the public–private balance be designed to ensure equity and efficiency? The answer to these questions challenged the welfare state as envisaged in the Swedish model or by reformers like [William] Beveridge, but the desirability of the welfare state in some form would remain inviolate.[163]

---

[162] For inter-generational connections among community based programs, it is important to see Vista and AmeriCorps or Job Corps as legatees from the New Deal initiatives such as the Civilian Conservation Corp. See Melissa Bass, *The Politics and Civics of National Service: Lessons from the CCC, Vista and AmeriCorps*, (Washington, D.C.: Brookings Institution Press 2013).

[163] Richard Pomfret, *The Age of Equality, the Twentieth Century in Economic Perspective*, (Cambridge: The Belknap Press of Harvard University Press, 2011), 108.

CHAPTER FOURTEEN: PHILOSOPHY NEEDS HISTORY

The thread of serious thinking about politics or political theory runs unevenly through the account we are sketching of history since Rousseau and the French Revolution. At times, it is plainly visible in the social events of revolt or repression or in times of financial crisis and scarcity.

At the height of the Cold War, a pair of divisive issues lay uneasily across American cities and campuses. Both the heat generated by the Civil Rights movement and the devastating war in Vietnam brought out wave after wave of protest, as well as calls for reform and greater accountability for national polices. Around the same time, though LBJ decided not to seek re-election in 1968, his reform-minded administration and the Democratic Congress made several bold moves in social legislation, as we've discussed, adopting Medicare, the Civil Rights Acts of 1964 and '65, and the Equal Employment Opportunity Commission (EEOC).

British thinker Bernard Williams, in his 1976 essay "The Moral View of Politics," looked back and noticed the "moribund condition of political philosophy" and suggested that "[l]iving political philosophy ... needs a context of political urgency, and the decline of political philosophy in the Fifties and early Sixties was ... a phenomenon of a period of political stagnation, one which prematurely saluted the end of ideology."[164] After that period of quiescence or complacency, Williams suggests, serous political conflict

---

[164] Williams was referring to Daniel Bell and his 1965 book by that title. The prematurity of Bell's claim found a distinctive echo a generation later, at the end of Soviet Union. See Francis Fukuyama, *The End of History and the Last Man*, New York: Free Press, 1992). Both books reflected a kind of self-satisfaction about liberal democracy and its staying power. Bell represented the discipline of sociology; Fukuyama political philosophy.

would revive philosophy, as we saw in mid-century America. The Vietnam war raised fundamental questions about the legitimacy of warfare, of compulsory service in that war, of civil disobedience, and similar questions about racial equality "which in the late 1960s unsettled conservative belief that [such inequalities] had gone away and liberal faith that they gradually [would] do so...."[165]

Williams's views mirror those of Sanford Lakoff's, from the previous decade, lamenting the depleted state of his field of political philosophy. While Lakoff published well before John Rawls and Robert Nozick made their major contributions to the field, Williams not only sees, but celebrates, their contributions to the revival of the genre.[166]

A renewed vitality in political philosophy owed more to the social and political ferment of the late 1960s than to a regeneration from within the discipline. Until then, in Williams's view, philosophy—particularly in Britain and the United States—suffered from a steadfast commitment to the separation of fact from value. Only when writers like Rawls and Nozick broke that taboo in the early '70s did the scope of serious political thought enter the mainstream. Both Rawls and Nozick chose to start with moral intuitions, like fairness in Rawls's case and in Nozick's, the presumption of legitimacy in existing ownership. Both build fairly elaborate arguments for certain kinds of social choices, preserving the distinctive individualistic and moral dimensions in them. Moreover both Rawls and Nozick, commendably in Williams's view, opened up the space for larger theoretical structures than was the norm previously.

Even so, the transformation was only partial. Rawls and Nozick (by the time of Williams's writing) limited themselves to thinking about society in abstraction from concrete social conditions of the time, disregarding significant divisions of the social sciences. Using economics and "decision theory" as their handmaidens meant that their arguments could be carried on a high

---

[165] Bernard Williams, "The Moral View of Politics," in *Essays and Reviews, 1959-2002*, (Princeton: Princeton University Press, 2014), 119.

[166] Sanford Lakoff, a Harvard-trained political historian, notes the decline of political philosophy in the 1950s. Bernard Williams, of Oxford, writing as a philosopher, largely attributes that decline to the influence of the analytic tradition then dominant in the Anglophone world. The other two men helped break that spell with their books of the 1970s, challenging both the then-dominant tradition and effectively debating each other on the competing claims of liberalism versus a new defense of conservatism. In fact, their competitive works—*A Theory of Justice*, by Rawls, and *Anarchy, State, and Utopia*, by Nozick—spawned much of the revival of political philosophy for the remainder of the twentieth century. The ideal of equality figures prominently in their works and the literature they induced.

level of abstraction, avoiding the more rough and tumble debate we might expect, say from the Op-Ed page. By not using the fields of sociology and social anthropology, they sidestepped the pervasive anxiety about "our current moral priorities" within those fields. We "understand too much in historical and social terms about the origins of our moral sentiments and conflicts," Williams argues, to be able to accept a purely abstract structure of principles however well internally harmonized it may be. It is the very conflict with regard to moral sentiments that calls for more from such writing.

How in particular do we see the link—in actual public events, protests as well as policy initiatives—of the time and the outpouring of writing since then? Let's start with the EEOC and OEO, which both built on the core concept of "equality of opportunity," a catch-phrase seriously pursued in the time of L.B.J.

If we are to move beyond R. H. Tawney's "fig leaf" caricature of the idea, must we not ask, as economist Amartya Sen has done, "equality of what?" Frequently, writers have answered that for the ideal to mean much at all, beyond basic legal and political equality of rights, we must see some observable improvement in individual wellbeing. R. H. Tawney certainly thought that way.

Juxtaposed to this overlay of contemporary writing is the bold proposition of Robert Nozick, who also wrote in the mid-1970s, seemingly in reaction to both Rawls and Bernard Williams. Nozick argues that any policy of promoting re-distribution has to contend with the need to justify altering existing institutions or patterns, like *my* land, *my* income, or *my* investments. In other words, Nozick postulates that any public policy that has a distributive intent to it, such as higher rates of taxes for some or affirmative action in college admissions for others, necessarily has an implicit RE-distributive quality. He argues that we must take society as it has been constituted, unless and until we see some sort of illegitimate acquisition on the part of those now holding those things. It seems fair to say that views like this are not new to the debate about equality as an ideal, given that they represent the arguments of conservatives since, oh, at least Herbert Spencer.

Much of the scholarly writing since Nozick has blunted the conservative claims for vested property rights by more or less skirting the challenge of a desirable distribution of material or economic goods. Thomas Nagel in 1977 argued that at least one view of the intrinsic value he calls "communitarian of equality" has to do with fostering right relations among the members of society—a society that recognizes the formation of fraternal attitudes and sympathies. Presumably, what follows from those right relations will adequately explain or defend any changes in distributional patterns of material goods. One implication of Nagel's point is that recognized, mutual respect characterizes the relations among members of a community results in, for example, fair wages and social mobility and tolerance for differences in religion or race.

Michael Walzer has offered an extended justification of Nagel's idea in his 1983 book, *Spheres of Justice*. His core contention suggests that we should not seek a perfect order of even distribution of all social goods, but aim for making sure within the culture of particular societies that some or all those goods are not dominated by any group or groups. The history of movement in the direction of a more equal society has to do with challenging every experi-ence of subordination of some by others. "Men and women are one another's equals ... when no one possesses or controls the means of domination...[T]he means of domination are [or have been] differently constituted in different societies. Birth and blood, landed wealth capital, education, divine grace, state power—all these have served at one time or another to enable some people to dominate others."[167]

Iris Marion Young confronts Nozick's main point by calling attention to his neglect of the social structure and institutional context that brought about an existing distributive pattern of benefits and burdens of citizens in the first place. And, in agreement with Nagel and Walzer, she argues that the starting point for a conception of social justice, one in which equality is an ideal, should revolve around the concepts of domination and exploitation and not on the distribution of social goods.[168]

When Ronald Dworkin coins the concept of "ethical individualism" in his essay, "Do Liberty and Equality Conflict?" he captures a major shift in writing philosophically about ideals. After Rawls, and even more so after Dworkin, the need to justify ideals in democratic societies in terms of human nature or its close relatives such as the social contract or natural rights simply subsides. The foundation has become implicit or taken as self-evident in this genre, and the discussion or commentary while more abstract, remains grounded in stories of contemporary experience.

Dworkin identifies two fundamental principles "very widely accepted in contemporary humanist societies," which together make up his "ethical

---

[167] Michael Walzer, *Spheres of Justice: A Defense of Pluralism and Equality*, (New York: Basic Books, 1983), xiii.
[168] Iris Marion Young, "Displacing the Distributive Paradigm," in *Equality*, edited by David Johnston, (Indianapolis: Hackett Publishing Co., 2000), 243-4.

individualism."[169] The first—the principle of equal value—holds that it is "intrinsically, objectively, and equally important that human beings lead successful lives."[170] This does not mean that "all human beings are in fact equally good or equally worthy of respect. "It insists only that it is equally important...that all human lives flourish."[171] J.S. Mill would agree, although his brand of individualism did not use the qualifier "ethical," a modifier that Dworkin fully exploits.

Early in his career Mill was in thrall to Jeremy Bentham's idea that socially-averaged flourishing supported the greatest good for the greatest number. Dworkin does not share that view. The second principle—special responsibility—requires that all individuals must commit to or accept that they must strive to live a life of flourishing, whatever their pursuits; or to borrow a phrase from a 1990s Army recruitment campaign, "Be all that you can be." Moreover, this principle of responsibility extends to support of a social environment that encourages and respects that commitment, solidifying the ethical dimension of Dworkin's individualism.[172]

With these principles in mind, Dworkin sees no necessary conflict between liberty and equality. For, "we cannot interpret the great Enlightenment virtues of liberty and equality...in isolation from one another. We must interpret each...in the light of what we think about the other."[173] Dworkin has worked through these ideas in contemporary debates about mechanisms for resource allocation or re-distribution, such as taxes and public support of medical care, something we will discuss in the next chapter.

T.M. Scanlon goes even further: "This aim—the ideal of a society in which people all regard one another as equals—has played a more important role in radical egalitarian thinking than the idea of distributive justice which dominates much discussion in our time."[174] Really? How is that possible? Isn't this claim built on such a broad base that it's almost impossible to compare conditions over time or measure particular aspects of instances of inequality? What, for instance, do gender income differentials have in

[169] Ronald, Dworkin. "Liberty and Equality Conflict?" in *Living as Equals*, edited by Paul Barker, (New York: Oxford University Press, 1996), 42.

[170] Dworkin, "Liberty and Equality," 42.

[171] Dworkin, "Liberty and Equality," 42.

[172] Although I cannot claim that Dworkin ever acknowledged such a suggestion, his ideas appear to reflect a clear acceptance of Rousseau's version of the social contract. We owe something *to each other* as members of a self-governing society—at least, one based on the intrinsic respect due to each human being in it.

[173] Dworkin, "Liberty and Equality," 43.

[174] T.M. Scanlon, "The Diversity of Objections to Inequality," in *The Ideal of Equality*, by Matthew Clayton and Andrew Williams, (New York: Palgrave, 2002), 43.

common with race discrimination or wage dependency of manual laborers versus the security of tenured teachers in education? Isn't the larger aim so broad that it can be dismissed as utopian? How would we know when its conditions have been met? Did Rousseau have reason to believe that such conditions as Scanlon and the others have stipulated were present in Geneva when he lived there? He certainly implied as much in thinking about what that city-state possessed as a republican form of government compared to the kingdom of France and its landed aristocracy.

Scanlon, to be fair, surveys a range of ways in which thoughtful observers might object to inequalities of various kinds. And the quotation above underscores the importance of avoiding stigmatizing people based on differences in status—the "evil of treating people as inferior."[175] In other words, Scanlon's paper identifies a varied collection of inequalities and examines in what ways they are, or might seem, unjust.

Walzer's work emerges as a synthesis or virtual reservoir of much of the relatively recent scholarship on our subject. First, unlike many eighteenth century writers, drawing conceptions in blank—or without necessary application to any particular social order, Walzer claims that if the ingredients are not already contained, even if only implicitly, in our present day institutions and practices, then we are not likely to build a more equal society.

Some of these, he might add, appear explicit in form, such as the equal protection clause of the 14th Amendment. We find others scattered over the landscape of aspirational documents like the Declaration of Independence or Lincoln's Gettysburg Address. Still others occur in observer classics like Alexis de Tocqueville's *Democracy in America*, in which his keen eyes note the shared commonality of material conditions, which he sees as supportive of, if not directly producing, a kind of fraternal familiarity with each other in the Americans he met in different places. Few if any working men, for example, took off their caps when talking with their foreman or employer, as they would have done in the Europe of his time.

Second, Walzer bids us to let go of the favored conceptualizations of natural law, the state of nature, human nature, and of a social contract. Implicitly he might consider all of these terms artifacts of traditional philosophy, and therefore not so much refuted as omitted from present-day preoccupations. Another way of "doing philosophy," Walzer suggests, involves "interpret[ing] to one's fellow citizens the world of meanings we share,"[176] implying that we need not search for an avowed moral catalyst to commit

---

[175] Scanlon, "Diversity of Objections," 43.
[176] Walzer, *Spheres*, xiv.

to address inequalities. There is, he insists, that equivalent of moral force already present, impelling its own practical recognition in how we treat each other.

Third, he chooses to speak not in terms of rights of any kind but in terms of "shared conceptions of social goods"[177] that makeup the complexity of our modern life.[178]

By "spheres," Walzer means to identify by category of social goods how their production and sharing has worked in practice. In other words he assumes that each social good is produced and shared in differing ways, through identifiable institutions. This means that we cannot reliably judge their status as if they were all created, sustained or modified in identical ways. Here is one example of Walzer's meaning in separating the spheres this way. In the sphere of wealth—income is produced typically by the actual effort and personal attributes of intelligence and learned capacities. The relative distribution of wealth should be confined to those qualities and not, for example, on an employee's religious identification. In the sphere of citizenship, the exercise of its rights such as voting ought not to depend upon the member's wealth.

The list may grow as the course of social life itself expands and becomes more complex as it certainly had done since Rousseau's time. These are the six that compose his listing, drawn from a reflective reading of Western civilization: *membership* in a community of some authority and power, i.e., what citizenship nominally implies in terms of basic security and communal provision historically illustrated; the sphere of *wealth*—money and what it can and cannot buy with special attention to the market place and determination of wages; *education*; the realm of *affection*—kinship and love; *religion*; and the sphere of *recognition*, positive as in honors and negative as in deprivation of liberty. The term "respect" is sometimes used as the equivalent of "recognition" as in the writings of Richard Reeves, an economist at the Brookings Institution.

Walzer's system is not free of ambiguity, of course, for certain social goods may indeed transcend the boundaries of the list he uses. A notable example is the on-going policy issue of how human health care ought to be

---

[177] Walzer, xiv.

[178] Essentially, people take on concrete identities because of the way they conceive and create, possess and employ social goods. And these are those that are valued by historic practice in the society we are examining, in our case the United States of America over time. Social goods are distributed in accordance with our shared understanding of their scope in identifiable realms of life.

assured. On the one hand, health care seems to be covered by the phrase we noted above, under the sphere of community membership, to wit: "basic security and communal provision." On the other hand the American experience we know is much more complicated than that and our history reveals a mixture of spheres impacted, not least wealth or income as through employer or individual insurance.

Here it begins to emerge why Walzer has no need to identify an explicit moral foundation for any of these social meanings. Why? Because it is not «ought-ness" that moves us, but, first and foremost, a studied perception of what social practices we collectively have endorsed. The basic quality of human and social relations that Walzer acknowledges, has been with us for a long time, certainly from the time of Rousseau and the French Revolution: the recognition of our common humanity. And yet, while manifestly different from one another individually, we are also demonstrably alike in many ways. Moreover, in those ways we have all, at one time and place or another, come to oppose conditions that permit hierarchies of domination. When any group or person possesses such power, the vision of equality is most compelling. Thus for Walzer, the root meaning of equality is negative: egalitarianism aims at eliminating not all social differences, let alone all personal distinctions, but those differences that permit one group to dominate fellow citizens. "The experience of subordination...lies behind the vision of equality," he contends.[179]

Finally, one more distinctive feature separates Walzer's ideas from those of his predecessors. Not only does he forgo "rightness" in terms of Kant's categorical imperative, but he eschews the more modern ethic of utilitarianism. While reforms that came about in the wake of J.S. Mill's ideas combined with those of Jeremy Bentham, have doubtlessly contributed to a less unequal social order since then, Walzer recognizes a lurking defect in that philosophy as a guide to a fair distribution of goods. He shies away from utilitarianism—the greatest good for the greatest number—for it contemplates a kind of science of administration applied by planners whose role would conceivably dominate. The process of social mediation of goods achieves its healthy balance against monopolies of domination through a more subtle art, an art of differentiation.

Here, Walzer's notion of various "spheres" of social and political life comes into play, along with the concept of distributive justice. The task for all of us, especially those who observe and report on such things, emerges as

---

[179] Walzer, xiii.

critical. To have a just distribution of social goods does not require an identical pattern over the whole of our social and political existence. Rather, it insists that we observe closely enough to discern trends toward domination. That can best be done by breaking down our complex social and political connections one sector at a time.

For example, we can distinguish the dynamics of membership in society—citizenship—from the processes supporting our personal security and material welfare, as well as from those that qualify our work place prospects, educational opportunities, and religious affiliations. But, sometimes the categories overlap. Walzer explicitly calls our attention to such zones of congruence, including, for example, the sphere of work that most of us do not want to do. If the work, say trash collection, is done by some of our poorest citizens, as it most certainly is, the work is not only poorly compensated but it comes with a stigma and lower than average self-esteem. In Rousseau's time, Walzer tells us, road building—experienced as the most degrading kind of work—was undertaken through a form of conscription or forced labor, imposed upon the poorest and weakest of the king's subjects.

Rousseau believed that all citizens of a republic must share in socially necessary work just as they share political life and military service, "if they are ever to be citizens of a self-governing community" of equals. "We know, Rousseau argued, that the republic [such as his own place of origin, the city-state Geneva] is in decay when it's citizens 'would rather serve with their money than with their persons.'"[180]

Walzer concedes that the sharing of work such as trash collection or home health care cannot readily extend beyond those already doing it, especially those marginalized in our society like many immigrants without special skills. But we can, he argues, recognize the ways to reduce social stigma enhance self-worth. He gives us the example of a member-owned cooperative association: the San Francisco Sunset Scavengers. For seventy plus years this self-directed group has contracted with the city to collect much or most of the trash. Members receive equal compensation even while some serve as leaders of the group on a rotating basis. Their work is still demanding but the pay is good and the morale high. Moreover, as one sociologist discovered, they have a higher safety record than the industry-wide average. "The success of the cooperative may owe something to the easi-

---

[180] Walzer, 171.

ness of the members with one another...They have made membership a good thing."[181]

Throughout most of the modern economy, the division of labor has developed differently, continually separating out rather than integrating the hardest sorts of work. This is especially true in the care we provide for the sick and old. There is no transforming such hard work, but we can make it less socially negative through unions and co-ops. With still relatively modest compensation, the industry can enhance conditions with greater job security, a rotation in assignments, and medical benefits. Those—or other— enhancements will likely raise the self-respect of the individual participants. Walzer theorizes that these marginal ways of change can make distinctive differences in the communal lives of the workers themselves. With that change comes some easing of the negative dominance, as he calls it, histori- cally tied to the jobs at the lowest rungs of society. The solidarity and energy of the workers themselves are both cause and effect in this newly re-imaged approach to work.[182]

Richard Reeves, an economist working at the Brookings Institution, has emphasized the singular importance of work in the American historical context. He finds—after basic and material equality—the work dimension of our social life, crucial to what he lists as the third kind of equality worth talking about—relational. Work builds respect among peers and self-respect in the individual. In today's America, Reeves claims, with the authority of data, that for a variety of reasons work is simply no longer central to the lives of many; we not only have underemployment but also unfulfilling work, with poor compensation and income differentials at large. Reeves offers a number of ways in which we, as a society, can rebuild—or replace—the central role of labor with other satisfactory ways to achieve respect in relationship to our fellow citizens. His ideas are broadly enough conceived to bring to mind the example above about the trash collection cooperative in San Francisco.

Bernard Williams seems to agree with Walzer in important ways. He has given us a glimpse of why or how he and Walzer seemingly follow a similar working model of concepts like equality and liberty. In "Why Philosophy Needs History," Williams points out that behind such concepts

---

[181] Walzer, 179. What is most socially distinctive in the experience of the Sunset Company is the way in which hard work is connected to other activities — in this case the meetings of the "stockholders" (as the bylaws refer to members), the debates over policy, the election of officers and new members. The company has also expanded into land-fill and salvage operations, providing new and diversified employment (including managerial jobs) for some of the members.

[182] Walzer, 174-77.

exists "a history of how people have come to think" of and use the terms.[183] Williams claims that not only do we not fully understand our political ideas or how we came to have them, we fail to recognize the distinctive meanings different generations have given them. The individualism of J.S. Mill in mid-nineteenth century is not the same as that of libertarians of the twentieth. Moreover, those meanings have sometimes followed divergent directions. The "estate tax" of the New Deal era (and earlier) has morphed into "death duties" disparaged within today's American conservatism.

History adds to our speculative thought about such concepts as equality, liberty and democracy—or even more imaginative sub-shoots of them like a social contract or state of nature—the realization, constantly to be re-learned, that these concepts have not always existed. They have evolved and still do. Witness, for example, the use of the concept of social contract as a clearly heuristic device in John Rawls's hands, versus the way Hobbes, Locke, or Rousseau use it. Their thinking implies, if not a more palpable sense of the concept, at least a greater consciousness of something that helped explain social and political decisions or practices of the remembered past. A shared platform, if you will, for observing traditions thought to be either desirable or inevitable or both.[184]

While Rawls makes a point of claiming no such myth in advancing his version of the social contract, the others—Hobbes, Locke, Rousseau—stay mostly silent on the matter of pre-historic reality. Yet Rawls does not reject them; neither does he revive them. Walzer and Williams, for their part, want us to remember them as important way stations on our way to seeing more clearly what we have thought as a kind of collective cultural heritage. Neither author bets that we or those who come after us will build on that heritage successfully. Yet they both seem to imply not trying would be a disservice.

Even the "invention of historical time," Williams tells us, was itself an intellectual advance.[185] An advance, he claims, because without that awareness of change and continuity, we are nonplussed when we discover, for example, that a democratic regime elsewhere does not necessarily lead to the kind of fairness and tolerance we expect in our own place or time.

The North African country of Algeria, for example, heir to more than one continuing cultural legacy, can help us more fully appreciate the point about

---

[183] Williams, *Essays*, 406-7.

[184] In the mind of another imaginative thinker of the Enlightenment like Adam Smith (1723-1790) such a "place" or device could work its way into the enduring vocabulary of a whole new profession—economics: the "invisible hand" of the market.

[185] Williams, 409.

change mixed with memory. Algeria's 1988 revolution against autocracy has not seen a comparable growth of those values we in the West associate with representative government and a pluralistic society. Being Muslim in Algeria still counts for more than other identities; press freedoms are still limited. Independence from French colonial rule has not delivered a full range of liberty's blessings. But that's likely true also of "mature" democracies, whatever their progression. It's just easier to see what's "missing" from them in the example of another culture or time.

Williams cautions against forsaking our commitment to, say, the value of individual freedom but rather add it to our store house of stories and accounts of how those values have fared in different places and times. He calls this weaving of philosophy and history a family tree of concepts and ideas. In that vein, contemporary Americans are not likely to abandon the reach for racial equality just because we now know more fully that the genealogy of the concept reveals its hollowness in pre-Civil War generations. We know that, now—not by magically intuiting it from an otherwise clear and simple narrative but by way of fleshing out the often obscured and incomplete narrative with greater detail. A richer weaving of history and critical reflection sustains us in the task, and that is why the writings of Walzer and Williams both are of signal importance.

Conclusion

The Weight of Four Decades

There is ample explanation for the surge in critical writing about *inequality* among economists. They are widely agreed: there has been a steady and increasingly rapid rise in incomes of relatively few Americans compared to stagnation in wages for most others for a generation. According to Thomas Piketty, "[s]ince 1980 ... inequality has exploded in the United States. The upper decile's share increased from 30-35 percent of national income in the 1970s to 45–50 percent in the 2000s—an increase of 15 points of national income."[186]

By contrast, Timothy Noah tells us, "during the previous five decades—from the early 1930s through most of the 1970s—the precise opposite had occurred. The share of the of the nation's income that went to the wealthy had either shrunk or remained stable."[187]

The comment of noted labor economist Robert Reich is equally compelling:

> For three decades after World War II, America created the largest middle class the world had ever seen. During those years the earnings of the typical American worker doubled, just as the size of the American economy doubled. Over the last thirty years, by contrast, the size

---

[186] Thomas Piketty, *Capital in the Twenty-First Century*, translated by Arthur Goldhammer. (Cambridge: Belknap Press of Harvard University Press, 2014), 294.

[187] Timothy Noah, The Great Divergence: America's Growing Inequality Crisis and What We Can Do About It, (London, New York: Bloomsbury Press, 2012), 1.

of the economy doubled again but the earnings of the typical America went nowhere.[188]

The same explanatory phenomenon holds where the income springs from salary and wages or from invested capital. As Nobel Laureate Joseph Stiglitz has reported, the disparities in income from capital set a much higher pace than those in wage and salary income, such that even after the Recession of 2008 "the top one percent own seven-eighths of capita income while those in the bottom 95 percent claimed less than three percent."[189]

Beneath the summary of inequality data, features of our history warrant explicit attention for fuller understanding. For example, the nature of economic organization and the corresponding character of work have changed steadily, albeit more rapidly in some periods than others, since the advent of the Industrial Revolution. Chapter Four provides some of that story. From economies based on land and its cultivation by people who did not own any or much land to large manufacturing plants of European and American cities of the nineteenth century the shift has been from one form of capital asset to another. Having thus organized themselves into companies for the production of things, owners and their managers set about to control costs of production, especially payments to workers. The law mandating a minimum wage has become a veritable maximum by many employers— a practice particularly exploited during the unfriendly atmosphere of the 1980s that continues to the present time.

Manufacturers have used all kinds of inventions—like automation—to cut their costs over two hundred years of industrial revolution. The interest in and capacity of technical innovation has not slowed, resulting in the need, today, for fewer and fewer hands on the shop floors. Similarly, on the huge commercial farms, mechanization has replaced large numbers of human cultivators. Some economists do not put much weight on the impact of things like robots for elimination of all kinds of jobs. For them the story is more complicated than that. Even when factoring the loss of local jobs to offshore sites, there remains the puzzle of why more of America's continuing productivity margin has not found its way to better incomes for workers. Yet greater income continues to flow upward—to those who own or manage liquid capital, organized production, or rendered services.

---

[188] Robert Reich, *Saving Capitalism for the Many, Not the Few*, (New York: Borzoi Books, 2015), xi.
[189] Stiglitz, *Price of Inequality*, 8.

It does so because the return on capital generally, if not invariably, is greater than the rise in a country's productivity measured by GDP.[190] That's certainly the case in this second decade of the 21st century, and seemingly is true for both liquid capital—stocks, bonds, or other securities—and old fashioned asset capital—ownership in real property like factories, apartment houses, and other rent producing buildings. Piketty calls the accumulation permitted by that larger return from investment as opposed to wages a form of inherited wealth.[191] Before the 1980s, the United States taxed at "substantially higher rates" both income and estates.[192]

This reduction in federal income tax rates from the 1980s forward helped to trigger the parallel rise of income inequality. An explanation involves methods of corporate compensation to directors and managers. High tax rates gave such taxpayers less incentive to ask for greater pay and more incentive to accept other benefits like stock options, that they could conserve as a form of savings. Stock would only be taxed—at the lower capital gains rate—when sold, versus cash salaries, which were taxed when paid. Lower tax rates meant much less of the new pay would go to the IRS. It's not surprising, then, that these minders of our capital fortunes would seize the opportunity to advance their individual interests.

As a result of the 1981 and 1986 bills, during Ronald Reagan's administration, the top income tax rate was slashed from 70% to 28%.[193] The rates did not go back up substantially until the early budgets of the Clinton years when that president made budgetary deficits an issue; yet the G.W. Bush administration again cut rates.

Changes in tax rates of the magnitude experienced in the eighties did not happen without pressure. Ronald Reagan believed that growth of the economy would benefit all segments: "a rising tide lifts all boats." The expectation, albeit not one based on a tested economic model, was that higher-after-taxes incomes for owners and investors would encourage greater investment in new or expanded ventures resulting in more employment. In fact, Stiglitz says, "that didn't happen; growth in the era of deregulation and lower taxes was slower; and the country grew apart."[194]

---

[190] Piketty, *Capital*, 26-7.

[191] Piketty 26-7.

[192] Piketty, 499.

[193] Jeanne Sahadi, "Taxes: What people forgot about Reagan," CNNMoney.com, 12 September, 2010. https://money.cnn.com/2010/09/08/news/economy/reagan_years_taxes/index.htm#

[194] Stiglitz,157.

Stiglitz offers "socially constructed categories" of thought as another way to view the political innovation of the '80s and following. For example, when people associate with those who hold similar views, they construct belief systems: government is inefficient therefore it's better to keep any money not clearly serving a public purpose in private hands. And these beliefs take hold, often without debate or survey.[195] A comparable attitude among such social constructs submits that those who would benefit from greater public assistance are often undeserving because they do not work hard enough or have self-defeating habits.[196]

For every American voter who would tend to favor tax cuts for the wealthy there is another who would support having the rich pay both more per year, and more than those with less income.[197] Framing such issues becomes both a high political art and manifestly the craft of marketing experts. In this context it is understandable that some economists prefer to avoid the ideological standoff and talk instead about the pre-distributional structure of the economy—less about how taxes are spent and more about how taxable assets are produced in the first place, the process of wealth production.

Robert Reich breaks down that process into "building blocks" of the economy in his book *Saving Capitalism for the Many, Not the Few*. He argues that an erosion of "countervailing power" in the market core of our economy has taken place in this past forty years; forces that formerly kept income inequality less divergent have been weakened. Notable among these are labor unions. Various segments did manage to post gains through minimum wage legislation applicable to all workers whether in unions or not. "Small farmers got price supports for their crops and farm coops won exemption from the anti-trust laws, as did unions. Small retailers obtained protection against chains through state 'fair trade' laws, requiring wholesalers to charge all retailers the same price."[198]

Perhaps one of the clearest single pieces of evidence that unions have lost a substantial influence has to do with elections. According to Reich, "Democratic candidates no longer rely nearly as much on labor unions to finance

---

[195] Stiglitz, 156-62.
[196] Reporter Mickey Kaus claims to have observed something of the opposite persuasion in those he styles as "money liberals" in *The End of Equality* (New York: Basic Books 1993).
[197] See Stiglitz,159-60, especially footnotes 27 & 28.
[198] Reich, *Saving Capitalism*, 170. Reich further notes the widespread retreat or shrinkage of such groups or their power in an age when so many of us are just too busy to join. Robert Putnam's book *Bowling Alone: The Collapse and Revival of American Community*, (New York: Simon & Schuster, 2000), comes to mind with its fuller picture of decline in citizen participation in volunteer groups of all kinds, including work-place unions.

their campaigns as they do on wealthier individuals."[199] Contributions from such individuals along with those of big companies and trade associations have grown hugely, especially since the Supreme Court invalidated a statute regulating campaign financing. In the 2012 election, according to Reich, the Koch brothers themselves spent more than $400 million, a sum more than twice the political spending of the ten largest labor unions put together.

Joseph Stiglitz provides another indication of labor's decline in the U.S. Membership in unions has declined by fifty percent in the last thirty years. Whereas the initiatives of the New Deal under FDR encouraged unionization by providing federal protection for organizing public efforts in this field more recently have actively discouraged it. President Reagan ended the air controllers strike in 1981 by simply firing all the union members, something Reich considers a "critical juncture in the breaking of the strength of unions"[200] (65). In the wake of that move, state legislatures have added additional barriers, the so-called Right to Work Laws, that allow companies to stop collecting union dues from their employees, cutting off unions' primary means of support. Without some means to support their collective activities, a union finds it almost impossible to elicit a majority vote in a workplace, effectively shutting them out. Stiglitz's considers the praise some economists give to a "flexible labor market" as based on myth. In his view, it ignores the evidence of greater job performance and safer conditions in businesses in which a majority of employees have approved a union.[201]

The countervailing power of social groups at large but especially unions can also be seen in a somewhat larger frame. The very structures of employment have changed. For example, fewer manufacturing plants exist in the U.S. than a generation ago. And some of the larger companies focus less on the primary production of goods than distribution of things made all over the world. Amazon is a prime example.

It is not obvious why this kind of work should be less amenable to unionization—handling many, many packages of goods to be delivered in bundles instead of hammering, stamping or bolting metal parts together for a washing machine, for instance. Yet the record seems plain enough: Amazon's work force organization has been one of individualization. Employees are part-time and thus exempt from minimum wage laws. Or, as in the case of Uber drivers they are classed as "independent contractors" and similarly out

---

[199] Reich, 173.
[200] Stiglitz, 65.
[201] Stiglitz, 65.

of reach of traditional workplace benefits like insurance and hour limits on work.

Structural changes in the kinds of work we do in our modern economy impact what one economist has recently termed the "emerging face of the American working class." Men in hard hats standing before factory gates or with coal- blackened faces exiting the mines no longer represent much of the working class. According to Binyamin Applebaum, today we see the emerging faces of women—Latinas and women of color—keeping our children or caring for the personal needs of our shut-in parents.[202] We could add to this list a veritable army of men, and numbers of women, who drive the trucks moving goods to market. Drivers' earnings are generally higher than the average worker's, and likely that reflects some countervailing power left in the old Union of Teamsters from an earlier time.

The decline of the old working class has meant both an economic triumph for the nation and a personal tribulation for many of the workers. Technological progress has made American farms and factories more productive than ever, creating great wealth and cutting the cost of food and most other products. But the work no longer requires large numbers of workers. In 1900, factories and farms employed 60 percent of the work force. By 1950, a half-century later, those two sectors employed 36 percent. In 2014, they employed less than 10 percent.[203]

Those of us past working age recognize the travails of some common service jobs like restaurant servers or hotel and home clearers for example. Barbara Ehrenreich in her 2001 classic book *Nickel and Dimed; On (Not) Getting by in America* has given us her personal experience of trying to live on a minimum wage in such work. Whatever the worksite, the pay is too little, the hours inflexible and the benefits nonexistent. Nonetheless workers have the saving grace—though lacking any organized way to be in touch with each other—that sometimes one of their own might take a shift, so staying home sick only means losing a day's pay, rather than losing the job.

Sarah Kessler, a reporter at *Quartz*, has described how the character of work changes without an actual worksite—not a factory, nor motel or restaurant. In *Gigged: The End of the Job and the Future of Work*, she describes the world our "millennials" have joined if not created. They dream of being their own bosses, of work more varied or interesting than an office from

---

[202] Binyamin Applebaum, Introduction, "The Jobs Americans Do," The Future of Work, *The New York Times Magazine*, February 23, 2017, https://www.nytimes.com/2017/02/23/magazine/the-new-working-class.html.
[203] Applebaum, Introduction.

nine-to-five without a supervisor on scene, and of having the freedom to work when they wish to.

Working from home with the skills to match the needs, say, of computer programming or data processing, fits this mold, and some of Silicon Valley's spinoffs have certainly brought attention to that kind of gainful employment. Yet, without a direct link to consumers wanting their particular services, this kind of work typically depends on individual organizing and marketing activity something, in the traditional economy would come from a now-absent corporate entity. The variables of the market will have as much or more impact as they might expect from staying in a traditional nine-to-five. Plus, most likely classified as "independent contractors," they lack both company benefits and the legal protections of state and/or federal labor laws. As "professionals" they assume all risks, including health or business insurance.[204]

Kessler amply illustrated the more newly created realm of *Uber* drivers who require no special educational skills. And while they don't get to stay at home, they can drive when they want, in their own cars. The company benefits by having no overhead for fleet maintenance and much lower personnel costs, as the company only pays drivers for pre-listed customer rides. The terms of the service offered, however, emerge as problematic for drivers. For example, corporate decides whether there's an automatic tip added to the standard fee, or if local demands require fee adjustments.[205] Uber drivers, as independent contractors, have no resort to join a union, to negotiate with corporate leadership, and practically, the confidential nature of driving records renders joint action problematic.[206]

Two insights in Kessler's study stand out. One, she sees the innovation of automated services—whether in city transport services like Uber or the programming farm-out system of a Google mega company—as part of a longer term process toward greater efficiency (likely greater returns to investors, as well) in the economy but without any very clear understanding of how the human impact of that efficiency will be acknowledged beyond the limited 'safety net' we established in much different material circumstances.

---

[204] Sarah Kessler, *Gigged: The End of the Job and the Future of Work*, (New York: St. Martin's Press, 2018), 95-8.

[205] Kessler, *Gigged*, 66.

[206] Very recently there have been initiatives forming such groups, like GigWorkersCollective (GWC) and Rideshare Drivers United (RDU), that meet such challenges through turning off the apps of drivers at intervals or failing to respond to a call for a particular gig, the "digital equivalent of a work stoppage." See "All Worked Up," *The Economist*, May 9 2020, 60.

Old age, child rearing, health maintenance—none of these have clear niches in the millennials' vision of the perfect job.

Why do those things have to be tied to jobs at all? Why do we think of both things at the same time? One of Kessler's consultants foresees that the labor market will become a collection of work assignments looking for workers, not job seekers looking for employment. "If you're a software developer, this is easy to envision. But if you're a truck driver, it's not clear what those tasks would look like."[207]

Robert Reich's inventory of conditions undermining countervailing power includes more than the newly emergent shape of work. There is a part played in the national elections; this is not surprising to political scientists but perhaps it is to some economists. He skewers the "concentration of wealth and income" for the influence that it has in the financing of political campaigns. With the single decision in 2010 of *Citizens United v. Federal Elections Commission* declaring corporations as persons, the Supreme Court held Congress could no longer restrict these entities formed for profit making from "speaking" through direct contributions to those campaigning for public office. Reich decried this development as "accelerating a vicious cycle in which large corporations and wealthy individuals pay to shape the rules of the game, thereby becoming even richer and having even greater influence over the rules' of our economic life."[208]

Restoring some degree of countervailing power in our economy at what Reich calls "pre-distributional" levels would by itself reduce a lot of income inequality. To determine a fair and sufficient level of income taxes for the whole range of functions the government performs would need an entirely separate inquiry. In other words, the scope and character of welfare benefits to people of very limited means would become a function of that additional step and not a factor in addressing structural changes in the first place. The social safety net needs to be adequate, but it does not have to bear the burden of the built-in biases of our over-all economy.[209]

Another notable "pre-distributional" adjustment to alleviate inequality affects the basic cost of living. A change in patent law to shorten the long exclusive ownership now available to pharmaceutical companies on drugs in demand for treatment of acute diseases would lower corporate profits, yes, but noticeably benefit a great many ordinary people. The contemporary condition of high drug costs is constantly before us. Consider the TV adver-

---

[207] Kessler, 245.
[208] Reich, 179-80.
[209] Reich, 169, 193.

tisement of at least one drug company that advises viewers who are unable to afford their product to ask for assistance: "Astra Zeneca may be able to help." Big pharma's price adjustment for the needy may make for good corporate public relations, but is it truly in the public's interest to have to ask for it?

Reich also proposes returning anti-trust law to the larger purposes once envisioned, reducing the political influence of large aggregates of economic power. Thus the old laws would experience a rebirth of power to break up cable monopolies and those controlling credit cards, the size of hospital chains, and the market power of high tech companies.[210] Similarly, contracts binding employees and others (like credit card holders) to arbitration for settling claims rather than using the courts would be prohibited by law.[211]

Redefining fraud to include a form of insider trading not presently illegal would prohibit companies from buying back their own shares to pump up their value in the stock market. Adjusting bankruptcy law could allow individuals with unmanageable student debt or mortgage debt on solo homes to refinance them giving them more leverage with lenders.[212]

Reich also advocates amending the minimum wage law to approximate some higher degree of the median wage in the industry or service sector and allow workers in low earning sectors like retail chains, hotels and hospitals to form unions across the entirety of their outlets. Workers at an individual franchise of McDonald's could join the voices of everyone who works at a McDonald's, regardless of location.[213]

Broader perspectives on income inequality often stress the great gaps between those in the higher ranges, with the most striking growth, and those more numerous of us in the lower to middle ranges, struggling with stagnating wages. A slightly narrower perspective, and perhaps more useful in the near term, comes from Richard Reeves. In his 2017 book *The Dream Hoarders*, he focuses a bright light on the biases built into the advantages that upper middle income citizens enjoy. Parallel to the barriers Reich finds "baked into the building blocks of our economy," these barriers seem equally powerful—deeply imbedded in our everyday culture alongside the economy.[214] Many silently take several core patterns for granted.

---

[210] Reich, 193.

[211] Reich, 194.

[212] Reich, 111-14.

[213] Reich, 194.

[214] Richard V. Reeves, *Dream Hoarders*, (Washington, D.C.: Brookings Institution Press, 2017), 155.

One crucial pattern that partially predetermines inequality begins with our zip codes. Zoning, a sort of grandfather of discrimination, was built on racial exclusion, and in more recent times it has affected the funding of public schools. The core of Reeves's critique shows how the ideal of equal opportunity is constantly thwarted by those in the top twenty percent who, at nearly every turn, favor their own children with access to private schools when the local public schools are underfunded and underperforming. Then the twenty-percenters give their children a more likely way to enter a college of high selectivity, followed by the graduate schools of note and so on to the internships at the very curbside of great jobs. This kind of escalator-effect of wealth, or greater-than-average income, tends to perpetuate a class of inherited advantage.

The wealth at this near-top of the pile does not produce poverty or lower income itself but it far more likely limits upward mobility in our society.[215] For Reeves, this is the greatest affront to our claim of a meritocracy based on individual grit and willingness to work hard. He acknowledges we do have some indicia of merit-based advancement, emphasizing both native intelligence and a willingness to use it, and so to that extent we have a kind of competitive market in jobs, even smart jobs. The drawback, however, is that the market is not competitive enough. There's little to insure a "level playing field" for those who, from earliest childhood, do not get to show up at the start of the game, when children and young adults cultivate personal attributes of intelligence and grit in the real competition for success.[216]

While the incidence of downward mobility, children of affluence "falling out" of the upper middle class, is statistically rare—less so in the lower rungs of the middle class—Reeves maintains that the opposite is characteristic of our age. A person born into disadvantage is, in America, far more likely to remain there in adulthood. Reeves's data indicate that the U.S. has more class rigidity than Europe, including the United Kingdom.[217] He asks his readers to consider the effect of rethinking John Rawls's "elegant, contract-based approach to social justice" in which participants, imaginatively, prepare to construct a government or governmental program based on fairness.[218] Instead of suspending our knowledge of who *we* are or will be, imagine that we do not know what conditions our children or grandchildren

---

[215] Reeves, *Dream Hoarders*, 74.
[216] Reeves, *Dream Hoarders*, 76.
[217] Reeves, *Dream Hoarders*, 58.
[218] Reeves, *Dream Hoarders*, 71.

will enjoy and construct our democratic model that way. It is, Reeves writes, his "intuition ... that upper middle class adults would be more supportive of redistributive policies and institutions if they were less certain where their own children ... were going to end up."[219]

Toward that end, Reeves concludes, our goal should be "to narrow the gaps in the accumulation of human capital in the first two and a half decades of life."[220] This would mean, among the more obvious steps, one, reducing unwanted pregnancy rates; two, narrowing the parenting gap; three, getting the best teachers to work in weaker schools; four, making college funding more equal.[221]

Specific to the "opportunity hoarding" at the heart of his book, Reeves makes three proposals: curb exclusionary zoning, open up college admissions, and reform internships by reducing the chances for the wealth and voice of parents to play the part they have now.

What makes Reeves's personal background as a transplanted Brit makes his thinking particularly persuasive. He admits to being "almost absurdly proud" of his new passport.

> But it has taken a while to figure out why... I have come to realize that what really draws me ... to America is the nation's spirit of openness and promise of social equality. I always hated the snobbery and class distinctions of the United Kingdom. But the harder I have looked at my new homeland, the more convinced I have become that the American class system is hardening, especially at the top. It has, if anything, become more rigid than in the United Kingdom. The main difference now is that Americans refuse to admit it.[222]

A note of modest optimism in Reeves's book reminds us that we can be inspired by examples in our own history. The Progressive Era's self-criticism, as he calls it, could lead us "once again to share rather than hoard, the American dream."[223] If there's any degree of uncertainty, if not demonstrable vulnerability, among the top twenty percent as to their children's or grand-

---

[219] Reeves, *Dream Hoarders*, 72.
[220] Reeves, *Dream Hoarders*, 124.
[221] Reeves, *Dream Hoarders*, 124.
[222] Reeves, *Dream Hoarders*, 155.
[223] Reeves, *Dream Hoarders*, 156. Reeves could also have flagged other such eras in American history when "sharing" was more actively promoted than now: The New Deal of 1930s (Chapter Ten), World War II (Chapter Eleven) and the Great Society of the 1960s (Chapter Twelve).

children's chance at success, Reeves suggests in this book, the voice and influence of that powerful demographic can make the difference.

Reeves's work of economics possesses something of the soul of philosophy we see in the scholarship of the late Ronald Dworkin (1931-2013). In his magisterial work *Sovereign Virtue: the Theory and Practice of Equality* (2000), Dworkin sees equality as the "endangered species of political ideals" that we dare not turn our backs on:

> For no government is legitimate that does not show equal concern for the fate of all those citizens over whom it claims dominion and from whom it claims allegiance. Equal concern is the sovereign virtue of political community...and when a nation's wealth is very unequally distributed, as the wealth of even very prosperous nations now is, then its equal concern is suspect.[224]

How that "sovereign concern" may be carried out, albeit under a variety of policies and practices, we tried to demonstrate in Chapter Thirteen. Dworkin's work figures there, too. Here we underscore just one of his most affirmative points: equality does not have to bend its knee to liberty. On the contrary, in a contest between them, liberty must lose![225] So if we care about liberty, we must look to see that equality itself is nourished. To the extent we can demonstrate that to one another in a free society, we can be confident that liberty is safeguarded.

The implication from Dworkin's message is that inequality of wealth or income is measurable by data whereas liberty's viability is subjective and rests on something other than material assets. What voters, or their elected leaders, decide to do about that kind of inequality is of course a separate question. Richard Reeves, claims "Americans are more tolerant of income inequality than the citizens of other countries."[226] That tolerance has endured for four decades so it is difficult to see how things could change. Individual habits die hard and so do, it seems, those of whole nations. Rousseau was not especially optimistic about our capacity to build institutions free from the hierarchy of class. He was skeptical, too, about that capacity in a mass society as large as a nation.

What might surprise Rousseau about America, however, is how much, though sporadically, the idea has been pursued through formal declarations, policies and laws. It is not that we failed to sustain all of these initiatives

---

[224] Dworkin, *Sovereign Virtue*, 1.
[225] Dworkin, *Sovereign Virtue*, 134.
[226] Reeves, *Dream Hoarders*, 58.

or start others but that the idea remained alive enough to move us at all. If he had been living when de Tocqueville visited and published *Democracy in America* two generations later, perhaps Rousseau would appreciate the roots equality's spirit had acquired. Of course that was a much simpler time, and the intervening history only became more complicated.

Even amid increasing complexity, our history suggests how particular crises themselves yield a certain clarity for the way forward. In revolutions, in depressions, and in war the national purpose is typically obvious for a time, even if the particular changes needed are not. The urgency for doing something calls for imagination and experiment.

The time of our study is like those, at least insofar as it reflects a sustained period of economic inequality. Yet there is more.

A Postscript from September 2020

Our present moment in history has suddenly become hugely more complicated as a global pandemic in six months has taken as many lives as our great wars. It threatens to reduce GDP to depression levels. It also has revealed how risks to health care have been exacerbated for the poor, people of color and so-called essential workers. For the United States there is another crisis of its own at this moment. A latter day confrontation with racism and its correlates among a range of disparities—including those affecting not just income and health but also the very basic guarantee of citizenship: equal justice under law.

The challenges of that constitutional standard have been continuous throughout our country's history not merely in trials, prisons or the death penalty but ever more obviously in the hands of police. The specter of a chronic inability to avoid excessive use of force in arresting or confronting people of color has generated sustained protest in city after city. The video images of these confrontations no doubt contribute to the urgency reflected in the protests. Perhaps, too, the scenes beyond the streets will also call out to us– inequalities in housing, jobs, schools and health care.

ACKNOWLEDGEMENTS

In a work that explicitly invokes the very notion of historic time, past and present somehow linked, it is scarcely possible to ignore a future beyond *this* time. At least it will be inhabited by loved ones who knew what we were attempting. From them we have taken the heart to imagine that what we have written might positively affect their world. To all of them we add an explicit acknowledgment for continued interest in and support for this book: Lucy, Dave and Robin; Kerry and Hall; Natalie, Chloe.

The future belongs of course to the living but also to those who will be *remembered*. My daughter Sarah Elizabeth's life was cut short before its time in 2018. She showed her interest in my work always, whatever turn it took. We talked about this very project long before it was actually commenced. And much else. Memories of those moments will resurface whenever I think about the ideas and people who inhabit this book.

For Algora Publishing's editors I express my appreciation for taking on this book project in the first place and praise in particular for the exceptional attention and patience of Andrea Secara, who was its shepherd throughout the months of its completion.

Finally, I acknowledge the invaluable help of my independent editor Sheri Malman. Her careful reading, questioning, and making suggestions came from a storehouse of literary craftsmanship. Less obvious a role was formatting the manuscript for final publisher submission. To the extent the completed book achieved organizational coherence or clarity of prose, Sheri's professional excellence is responsible. Any shortcomings that remain are mine alone.

BIBLIOGRAPHY

Abernethy, George L. *The Idea of Equality, An Anthology*. Richmond: John Knox Press, 1959.

Allen, Danielle. *Our Declaration, A Reading of the Declaration of Independence in Defense of Equality*. New York: Liveright Publishing Corporation, 2014.

Appelbaum, Binyamin. *The Economists' Hour*. New York: Little, Brown & Company, 2019.

_____. Introduction, "The Jobs Americans Do," The Future of Work, *The New York Times Magazine*. February 23, 2017. https://www.nytimes.com/2017/02/23/magazine/the-new-working-class.html.

Atkinson, Anthony B. *Inequality: What Can Be Done?* Cambridge: Harvard University Press 2015.

Bailyn, Bernard. *The Ideological Origins of the American Revolution*. Cambridge: Harvard University Press, 2017.

Barber, William J. *The Third Reconstruction: How A Moral Movement is Overcoming The Politics of Division and Fear*. Boston: Beacon Press, 2016.

Barker, Paul, ed. *Living as Equals*. Oxford, New York: Oxford University Press, 1996.

Bartel, Larry M. *Unequal Democracy: The Political Economy of the New Gilded Age*. Princeton: Princeton University Press, 2008.

Bass, Melissa. *The Politics and Civics of National Service: Lessons from the CCC, Vista and AmeriCorps*, Washington, D.C.: Brookings Institution Press, 2013.

Beatty, John. *Age of Betrayal: the Triumph of Money in America, 1865–1900*. New York: Knopf, 2007.

Blight, David W. *Frederick Douglass: Prophet of Freedom*. New York: Simon & Schuster, 2018.

Bloom, Allan. "The Education of Democratic Man: *Emile*." *Daedalus*, 107, No 3. (Summer 1978).

Brinkley, Allan. "Great Society" in *The Readers' Companion to American History*, edited by Eric Foner and John Arthur Garraty. New York: Houghton Mifflin, 2014.

Bronowski, J. and Bruce Mazlish. *The Western Intellectual Tradition: From Leonardo to Hegel*. New York: Harper & Row, 1975.

Burke, Edmund. *Reflections on the Revolution in France* in Vol. 24 of *The Harvard Classics*. New York: P.F. Collier and Son, 1909.

Calder, Angus. *The People's War, Britain 1939-45*. New York: Pantheon, 1969.

Colombia College Staff. *Introduction to Contemporary Civilization in the West, A Source Book*, Vol. II, "Robert Owen." New York: Columbia University Press, 1946.

Commins, Saxe, and Robert N. Linscott, eds. *Man and Man: The Social Philosophers*. New York: Random House, 1947.

Congressional Commission on Wartime Relocation and Internment of Civilians. *Personal Justice Denied*. Washington, D.C., 1982.

Correspondents of the New York Times. *Class Matters*. New York: Times Books, 2005.

Curtis, James and Lorne Tepperman. *Haves and Have-Nots: An International Reader on Social Inequality*. Upper Saddle River: Prentice Hall, 1994.

Dagger, Richard. *Civic Virtues: Rights, Citizenship and Republican Liberalism*. New York: Oxford University Press, 1997.

Damrosch, Leo. *Jean-Jacques Rousseau, Restless Genius*. Boston: Houghton Mifflin Company, 2007.

Dower, Robert S. "John Stuart Mill and the Philosophical Radicals." In *Social & Political Ideas of the Age of Reaction and Reconstruction* edited by F.J.C. Hearnshaw. New York: Barnes and Noble, 1949.

Dubois, W.E.B. *Black Reconstruction in America*. New York: Harcourt Brace, 1935.

Dworkin, Ronald. "Liberty and Equality Conflict?" in *Living as Equals*, edited by Paul Barker. New York: Oxford University Press, 1996.

_____. *Sovereign Virtue: The Theory and Practice of Equality.* Cambridge: Harvard University Press, 2002.

Dycus, Stephen, Arthur L. Berney, William C. Banks, and Peter Raven-Hansen. *National Security Law.* Philadelphia: Walters Kluwer, 2007.

Ehrenreich, Barbara. *Nickel and Dimed: On (Not) Getting By in America.* New York: Picador, 2011.

Flavell, Julie. *When London Was Capital of America.* New Haven: Yale University Press, 2011.

Foner, Eric. *Forever Free, The Story of Emancipation and Reconstruction.* New York: Vintage, 2005.

_____. *Reconstruction, America's Unfinished Revolution, 1863–1877.* New York: Harper & Row, 1988.

_____. *The Second Founding: How the Civil War and Reconstruction Remade the Constitution.* New York: W.W. Norton & Company, 2019.

Freeman, Samuel. *Rawls.* London, New York: Routledge, 2007.

Fink, Robert. "Homestead Act of 1682." Britannica. https://www.britannica.com/topic/Homestead-Act.

Fukuyama, Francis. *The End of History and the Last Man.* Washington D.C.: Free Press 1992

Gay, Peter. *The Enlightenment: An Interpretation,* Vol. II. *The Science of Freedom.* New York: Borzoi Books published by Alfred A. Knopf, 1969.

Gilbert, Felix. "Revolution." *Dictionary of the History of Ideas IV,* edited by Philip P. Wiener, New York: Scribner's, 1973.

Glendon, Mary Ann. *A World Made New: Eleanor Roosevelt and the Universal Declaration of Human Rights.* New York: Random House, 2002.

Godwin, William. *An Inquiry Concerning Political Justice.* Oxford: Oxford World Classics, 2013.

Graubard, Stephen R, Editor. "Rousseau in Our Time," *Proceedings of the American Academy of Arts and Sciences.* 107, No. 3, (Summer 1978).

Hartz, Louis. *The Liberal Tradition in America.* New York: Harcourt, 1991.

Hearnshaw, F.J.C., "Rousseau." In *Social and Political Ideas of Some Great French Thinkers of the Age of Reason.* Edited by F.J.C. Hearnshaw. New York: Barnes & Noble, 1950.

Hearnshaw, F.J.C. "Herbert Spencer and the Individualists." In *Social and Political Ideas of Some Representative Thinkers of the Victorian Age* edited by J.F.C. Hearnshaw. New York: Barnes and Noble, 1950.

Hitchens, Christopher. "Reactionary Prophet." *The Atlantic.* April, 2004.

Hofstadter, Richard. *Anti-intellectualism in American Life.* New York: Alfred A. Knopf, 1969.

Hunt, Lynn. *Inventing Human Rights, A History.* New York: W.W. Norton, 2007.

Isaacson, Walter. *Benjamin Franklin, An American Life.* New York: Simon & Schuster, 2003.

Israel, Jonathan. *A Revolution of the Mind: Radical Enlightenment and the Intellectual Origins of Modern Democracy.* Princeton: Princeton University Press, 2010.

_____. *Revolutionary Ideas, An Intellectual History of the French Revolution from the "Rights of Man" to Robespierre.* Princeton: Princeton University Press, 2014.

Johnson, Lyndon B. "Remarks Made at the University of Michigan, May 22, 1964." *Public Records of the Presidents, 1963–1964.*

Kaus, Mickey. *The End of Equality.* New York: Basic Books, 1992.

Kennedy, David. *Freedom From Fear, the American People in Depression and War, 1929–1945.* New York: Oxford University Press, 1999.

Kessler, Sarah. *Gigged: The End of the Job and the Future of Work.* New York: St. Martin's Press, 2018.

Lakoff, Sanford. *Equality in Political Philosophy.* Cambridge: Harvard University Press, 1964.

_____. *Ten Political Ideas That Have Shaped the Modern World.* Lanham: Rowman & Littlefield, 2011.

Lapore, Jill. *These Truths, a History of the United States.* New York: Norton, 2018.

Lechner, Ira D. "Massive Resistance: Virginia's Great Leap Backward." *Virginia Quarterly Review* 74 (Autumn 1998), 631-40.

Lilla, Mark. *The Shipwrecked Mind on Political Reaction.* New York: The New York Review of Books, 2016.

Mason, David S. *A Concise History of Modern Europe.* Lanham: Rowman & Littlefield, 2011.

Melzer, Arthur M. *The Natural Goodness of Man: On the System of Rousseau's Thought.* Chicago: University of Chicago Press, 1990.

McGerr, Michael. *A Fierce Discontent: The Rise and Fall of the Progressive Movement in America.* Oxford: Oxford University Press, 2003.

Mill, John Stuart. *The Subjection of Women*. Fairhope, AL: Mockingbird Classics, 2015.

_____. *Utilitarianism*. London: Longman, Green & Co., 1879.

Moran, Michael, "Emerson" *The Encyclopedia of Philosophy* Vol. 2. New York: Macmillan, 1967.

Mumford, Lewis. *The Culture or Cities*. New York: Harcourt, Brace and Company, 1938

Neiman, Susan. *Moral Clarity, A Guide for Grown-Up Idealists*. Princeton: Princeton University Press, 2009.

Noah, Timothy. *The Great Divergence: America's Growing Inequality Crisis and What We Can Do About It*. New York: Bloomsbury Press, 2012.

Noer, Thomas J. "M.L. King and the Cold War." *Peace and Change*. 22 no. 2. (April 1997). 111–131.

Nozick, Robert. *Anarchy, State and Utopia*. New York: Basic Books, 1974.

Pagden, Anthony. *The Enlightenment and Why It Still Matters*. New York: Random House, 2013.

Page, Francis M. "Robert Owen and the Early Socialists. " *Social and Political Ideas of the Age of Reaction and Reconstruction*, edited by F.J.C. Hearnshaw. New York: Barnes & Noble, 1949.

Paul, Ellen Frankel, Fred D. Miller, Jr., and Jeffrey Paul, eds. *Liberty and Equality*. Oxford: Basil Blackwell, 1985.

Philp, Mark. "Introduction." *An Enquiry Concerning Political Justice* by William Godwin. Oxford: Oxford World Classics, 2013.

Piketty, Thomas. *Capital in the Twenty-First Century*. Translated by Arthur Goldhammer. Cambridge: Belknap Press of Harvard University Press, 2014.

Pinker, Steven. *Enlightenment Now: The Case for Reason, Science, Humanism and Progress*. New York: Viking, 2018.

Pomfret, Richard. *The Age of Equality, the Twentieth Century in Economic Perspective*. Cambridge: The Belknap Press of Harvard University Press, 2011.

Putnam, Robert D. *Bowling Alone: The Collapse and Revival of American Community*. New York: Simon & Schuster, 2000.

Putnam, Robert D. and Lewis Feldstein. *Better Together, Restoring the American Community*. New York: Simon & Schuster, 2003.

Rawls, John. *Political Liberalism*. New York: Columbia University Press,1993.

_____. *A Theory of* Justice. Cambridge: Harvard University Press, 1971.

Reeves, Richard V. *Dream Hoarders*. Washington, D.C.: Brookings Institution Press, 2017.

_____. *John Stuart Mill, Victorian Firebrand*. London: Atlantic Books, 2007.

Reich, Robert B. *Saving Capitalism for the Many, Not the Few*. New York: Borzoi Books published by Alfred A. Knopf, 2015.

Robin, Cory. *The Reactionary Mind*. Oxford. New York: Oxford University Press, 2018.

Robinson, David M. ed. *The Political Emerson*. New York: Beacon Press, 2004.

Rogers, Daniel T. *Atlantic Crossings: Social Politics in a Progressive* Age. Cambridge: The Belknap Press of Harvard University Press, 1998.

Rosenblatt, Helena. *Rousseau and Geneva*. Cambridge: Cambridge University Press, 1997.

Rosenman, Samuel, ed. *The Public Papers and Addresses of Franklin D. Roosevelt*. New York: Random House, 1938–1950.

Rossi, Alice E., ed. *The Feminist Papers: From Adams to Beauvoir*. Boston: Northeastern University Press, 1988.

Rousseau, Jean-Jacques. *The Confessions of Jean Jacques Rousseau*. New Delhi: Pupa, 2000.

_____. *Emile*. Edited by P.D. Jimack. New York: Everyman Classics, 1974.

_____. *The Social Contract and Discourses*. Translated by G.D.H. Cole. New York: Barnes & Noble, 2007.

Saul, John Ralston. *The Unconscious Civilization*. New York: Free Press, 1995.

Scanlon, T.M. "The Diversity of Objections to Inequality." *The Ideal of Equality*, by Matthew Clayton and Andrew Williams. New York: Palgrave, 2002.

Schama, Simon. *Citizens: A Chronicle of the French Revolution*. New York: Vintage Books, 1989.

Schneewind, J. B. "John Stuart Mill." In the *Encyclopedia of Philosophy* edited by Paul Edwards. New York: Macmillan, 1972.

Sen, Amartya. *Inequality Re-examined*. Cambridge: Harvard University Press, 1995.

Shklar, Judith N. "Rousseau for Our Time." *Daedalus*. 107 (Summer 1978).

_____. "Jean-Jacques Rousseau and Equality." *Daedalus*. 107 (Summer 1978).

Smith, Adam. *The Theory of Moral* Sentiments. Amherst: Prometheus Books, 2000.

Stansell, Christine. *The Feminist Promise, 1792 to the Present*. New York: Modern Library, 2011.

Stanton, Elizabeth Cady. "The Destructive Male." Great Speeches Collection. *The History Place*. http://www.historyplace.com/speeches/stanton.htm

_____. *Eighty Years & More: Reminiscences 1814–1897* . London: T. Fisher Unwin, 1998.

Stiglitz, Joseph E. *The Price of Inequality*. New York: W.W. Norton & Company, 2012.

Sykes, Norman. "The Age of Reaction and Reconstruction, 1815–1865." In *Social and Political Ideas of the Age of Reaction and Reconstruction* edited by F.J.C. Hearnshaw. New York: Barnes & Noble, 1949.

Tawney, R.H. *Equality*. New York: Capricorn Books, 1961.

Thurow, Roger. "After 50 Years, Some Try to Lay the Ghosts Of Segregation to Rest," *The Wall Street Journal*, June 8, 1998.

Tribe, Laurence H. *American Constitutional Law*. New York: Foundation Press, 1978.

Waldron, Jeremy. *One Another's Equals, The Basis of Human Equality*. Cambridge: The Belknap Press of Harvard University Press, 2017.

Walzer, Michael. *Spheres of Justice, A Defense of Pluralism and Equality*. New York: Basic Books, 1983.

Weiss, Elaine. *The Woman's Hour: The Great Fight to Win the Vote*. New York: Penguin Books, 2018.

Wiener, Philip Paul, ed. *Dictionary of the History of Ideas*. New York: Charles Scribner's Sons, 1974.

Wilkinson, Richard and Kate Pickett. *The Spirit Level: Why Greater Equality Makes Societies Stronger*. London, New York: Bloomsbury Press, 2009.

Williams, Bernard. *Essays and Reviews, 1959-2002*. Princeton: Princeton University Press, 2014.

Wills, Garry. *Inventing America, Jefferson's Declaration of Independence*. New York: Vintage, 1979.

Wollstonecraft, Mary. *A Vindication of the Rights of Man*. Cambridge: Cambridge University Press, 1995.

_____. *A Vindication of the Rights of Woman*. Delhi: SWB Books, 2010.

Wood, Gordon. *The Purpose of the Past, Reflections on the Uses of History*. New York: Penguin, 2008.

Woods, Randall. *LBJ: Architect of American Ambition*. New York: Simon and Schuster, 2007.

Yellen, Eric S. *Racism in the Nation's Service: Government Workers and the Color Line in Woodrow Wilson's America*. Chapel Hill: UNC Press, 2013

Young, Iris Marion. "Displacing the Distributive Paradigm," in *Equality*, edited by David Johnston, New York: Hackett Publishing Co., 2000.

INDEX

Diderot, Denis, 16, 23
distributive justice, 21, 147, 150
Douglass, Frederick, 7, 8, 71-75, 77, 79, 102, 103, 107
Dubois, W.E.B., 7, 81
draft of World War II, 34, 69, 122
Dworkin, Ronald, 146, 147, 166

E

Eisenhower, Dwight D., 1, 117, 138
Emerson, Ralph W., 7, 63, 64
Enlightenment, Age of, 4, 16, 17, 23, 24, 29, 46, 51, 53, 61-63, 147, 153
Emile, 4, 5, 21-23, 50, 107
Equal Employment Opportunity Commission (EEOC), 137, 143, 145
equal protection of the law, 34, 77, 78, 91, 132, 148
estate tax, 153

F

Fair Labor Standards Act of 1938, 9, 117
Farmers' Alliance, the, 88
Federal Writers' Project, 116
feminism, 106-108
feudalism, 4, 5, 29, 40, 45, 57-61, 64
Fifteenth Amendment, 8, 71, 77, 79, 91, 102, 107
Financial Crisis of 1873, 88
Food Stamps, 141
Foner, Eric, 7, 81, 83, 85
Four Freedoms Address of FDR, 122
Fourteenth Amendment, 77-79, 91, 98, 132
Franklin, Benjamin, 23, 25, 34, 38, 68
Freedmen's Bureau, 82, 84

G

Gandhi, Mohandas, 128
Garrison, William Lloyd, 7, 71-73, 77, 79, 103

Geneva, 17, 118, 148, 151
Gilded Age, the, 8, 89, 97
Glendon, Mary Ann, 10, 109, 126
Godwin, William, 39, 51
George, Henry, 88, 89, 92
Gouges, Olympe de, 106
Grange, the, 88
Grant administration, 84
Great Depression, 8, 9, 11, 109, 111
Grimke, Angelina, 73, 75

H

Hayes, Rutherford B., 84, 87
Harrington, Michael, 141
Hartz, Louis, 61
Head Start, 140-142
Helvetius, Claude Adrieu, 23, 26, 51
Hearnshaw, F.J.C., 53
human capital, 165
hierarchies of domination, 150
Hitchens, Christopher, 40
Hobbes, Thomas, 19
Hofstadter, Richard, 97, 98
home front, 9, 123
Hoover, Herbert, 113, 121
Hopkins, Harry, 116, 118
Hull House (see also Settlement House), 7, 95, 97
Hume, David, 23, 60
Hutcheson, Francis, 23

I

Income Tax Amendment, 89
income tax rates, 157
individualism, 6, 7, 32, 33, 48, 58, 62, 63, 67, 108, 121, 146, 147, 153
Iron Curtain speech, 131, 135
Israel, Jonathan, 34, 106